Covert Surveillance and Electronic Penetration

Edited by
William B. Moran

Loompanics Unlimited
Port Townsend, WA

Covert Surveillance and Electronic Penetration
© 1983 by William B. Moran

Published by:
Loompanics Unlimited
P.O. Box 1197
Port Townsend, WA 98368

Typesetting and layout by Patrick Michael

Cover by Kevin Martin

ISBN 0-915179-20-2

PREFACE

The purpose of this book is to acquaint the general reader, as well as the law enforcement officer, with the techniques and equipment used in covert surveillance and electronic penetration. The material in this book has been gathered from various public domain sources, largely government reports, which, purchased separately, would cost the reader over $60.

The information has been completely reorganized for easier understanding, with all bureaucratic jargon and other superfluous material excised. To make reading easier, the text has been completely retypeset and new drawings commissioned where necessary. New information has been added where appropriate, to make this the best possible book.

The original sources of the information in this book are as follows:

Chapter 1, "Techniques of Shadowing and Tailing." Revised and edited from a US Army Technical Bulletin, "Techniques of Surveillance and Undercover Operations."

Chapter 2, "Night Surveillance Equipment for Law Enforcement." Edited and adapted from a report "Night Surveillance for Law Enforcement," by Donald T. Heckel and Salvatore L. Raia.

Chapter 3, "Electronic Eavesdropping Techniques and Equipment." Edited and adapted from a U.S Department of Justice Law Enforcement Assistance Administration report of the same name.

Chapter 4, "Wiretapping." Edited and adapted from a top secret report of the MITRE Corporation, "Selected Examples of Possible Approaches to Electronic Communication Interception Operations," and including some material from "Electronic Eavesdropping Techniques and Equipment."

Chapter 5, "Telephone Bugging." Edited and adapted from an anonymous report titled "Telephone Bugging."

It is hoped that this book will be of value to all concerned citizens, police officers and civilians alike.

William B. Moran
Detroit, Michigan
September, 1983

"I'll ask you, as a lawyer, if you do not think that surreptitious entry, or burglary, and electronic surveillance and penetration, constituted a violation of the Fourth Amendment."
— *Watergate Hearings*

CONTENTS

TECHNIQUES OF
SHADOWING AND TAILING

General

Surveillance is the planned observance of persons, places or objects. It is normally concerned with persons. Places and objects watched are generally incidental to the primary interest of seeking information about certain people.

Surveillance, whether by foot or vehicle, is predominantly an exercise of commonsense, ability, tact and ingenuity on the part of the surveillant, based on his training or education relative to human motivation and behavior both normal and abnormal. Carefully planned and properly executed surveillances can be of considerable assistance in an investigation; conversely, lack of preparation, poor timing, and unsound surveillance practices can be detrimental to an investigation.

Surveillance may be used to locate residences, business places, or other places frequented by persons of interest to the investigation, or places in which criminal activity is conducted or real evidence may be obtained. It is used to obtain information concerning the scope and nature of a person's activities. One important use of surveillance is checking on informers and their information.

The surveillant should have as much knowledge of the investigation as possible in order that he may accurately interpret the actions of the subject. He should also know the elements of proof of various crimes to enable him to know when the subject has gone far enough to warrant apprehension. The suspect may be kept under observation until he has thoroughly completed the crime he set out to commit, except those crimes which, if completed, would result in bodily harm to victims. Continued surveillances, even after all the elements of a crime have been completed, can be rewarding. The surveillant

1

should not be too anxious to make an apprehension. Wait and observe. After apprehension, additional contacts that the suspect might have made cannot be observed.

Surveillance activities must be recorded carefully. The use of detailed notes and logs, still and movie camera (often with special lenses, films and light sources), tape recorders, and miniature electronic listening devices must be considered and utilized appropriately.

Preparations

Identification of Subject. If the subject is unknown to the surveillant, the best method of identification is to have the subject pointed out to him to allow the surveillant to make his own observation. The surveillant should also be provided with a photograph and a detailed and accurate description of the subject. A photograph and detailed description of the subject's automobile should also be obtained at the initiation of the surveillance.

Appearance of the Surveillant. The surveillant's attire should be in harmony with the area or neighborhood or group in which the surveillance is to be conducted. It has been said that dress must be conservative, but if conservative dress is not the customary dress for the area it will be most conspicuous. The dress must blend with the environment so that if the subject sees the surveillant once or twice, or even more often, he will not be suspicious or have any lasting impression. The "disguise" shows that the investigator normally and naturally belongs in the surroundings in which he finds himself.

Appearance should not stop at just the manner of dress. Rings or other jewelry indicating professional status or societies may have to be discarded. If a ring is normally worn it should be replaced by an innocuous one, since the mark left on the finger would be visible and could arouse suspicion. A bulge in a coat or pocket indicating that a firearm is being carried may also be a giveaway. The surveillant should not have any unusual physical characteristics which might attract attention to him. Moreover, he should not reflect by his appearance or habits that he is a law enforcement officer.

Planning. When two or more surveillants are to be used, a complete understanding between them of the surveillance techniques to be used, and when, must be assured. Discreet signals should be arranged so that each surveillant will understand exactly what a given situation is, and proceed with plans previously formulated to cover them. While planning is important and essential, it must take second place to the adaptability and ingenuity of the surveillants. Surveillants should be chosen for their aptitude and resourcefulness. They must have poise, patience and endurance. Prior to initiating the surveillance, the surveillant should prepare and document a cover-story which will stand up under confrontation by the subject. This cover story should provide a reasonable excuse for being in the neighborhood involved and for participating in the activity undertaken.

Electronic Equipment. As part of the preparation and planning it may be advisable to consider the use of electronic equipment. For foot surveillance, transmitting and receiving devices can be easily secreted on the person without arousing suspicion. Transmitters can be concealed in packages, brief cases, or on the person. For vehicular surveillance, battery-operated transmitters are available that can be used as "homing devices" by planting them in or on a subject's car. Best results are obtained with these transmitters if they can be connected to the car's radio antenna, but various adapters are available for the most sophisticated installations. The device might be taped to the chasis of the car, placed in the sidekick panels, or under the dash. Consideration should be given to the importance of the case since these transmitters are fairly expensive and may be lost.

Binoculars and/or Metascope Equipment. The use of light-gathering binoculars and/or metascope equipment for night-time surveillances should be considered and utilized appropriately.

Basic Precautions

A surveillant should not make abrupt, unnatural moves from doorway to doorway, from tree to tree, or take other similar actions which are unnecessary and attract attention. Theatrical disguises such as false beards are impractical, hard to maintain and are easily detectable. The surveillant should never look directly into the subject's eyes. If a surveillant must look at the subject while facing him, he should look slightly behind him or at his feet. He should not appear too innocent. When in a dangerous neighborhood he should walk on the curb side of the sidewalk to preclude the possibility of being attacked from doorways or alleys, and to obtain the best observation vantage point. Inexperienced surveillants must overcome the tendency to believe that the subject has "made" (identified) them because he glances at them several times. The typography of the area in which the surveillance is to take place should be studied so that areas or objects that will deny or mark observation can be avoided. The surveillant should be aware of the location of cul-de-sacs or "dead end" streets or alleys so that he can avoid being trapped or discovered. Minor changes in outer clothing, hand-carried items, etc., may alter the overall impression and help to prevent recognition of the surveillant.

To discover surveillants, a subject may suddenly reverse his course, enter a dead-end street, board and suddenly depart from a public conveyance, or engage in a variety of other ruses which might produce unconventional behavior by possible surveillants. The surveillant may counter these ruses by adherence to approved surveillance techniques, and — whenever possible — by a thorough prior reconnaissance of the surveillance area.

Hotels, theaters, restaurants, elevators and public conveyances pose special problems to the surveillant. Generally, it is necessary to move closer to the subject when he enters hotels and theaters to preclude his leaving through the various exits. In restaurants, the surveillant should enter the restaurant behind the subject and locate himself to insure observation of the subject.

The surveillant should order a meal which can be quickly prepared. Should the subject depart before the surveillant is served, the surveillant should pay for his meal and leave. When the subject uses an elevator, the surveillant should use the same elevator. The surveillant does not announce a floor or selects the top floor, exiting behind the subject. The use of public conveyances by the surveillant is facilitated if the surveillant supplies himself with adequate small change or tokens in advance.

Types of Surveillance

There are two general types of surveillance: mobile and fixed. A mobile surveillance is sometimes referred to as "tailing" or "shadowing," and the fixed, as a "stakeout" or "plant." A mobile surveillance may be made on foot or by vehicle, and is conducted when persons being observed move from point to point and are followed by surveillants. A fixed surveillance is conducted when a person or activity remains in place, although surveillants may move from one vantage point to another in the immediate area.

Methods of Surveillance

Loose Surveillance. During loose surveillances, subjects need not be kept under constant observation. The surveillance should be discontinued if the subject becomes suspicious.

Close Surveillance. In close surveillances, subjects are kept under observation continuously and surveillances are maintained at all times, even if the subjects appear to become suspicious and openly acost the surveillants or accuse the surveillants of following them.

Combined Loose and Close Surveillance. Circumstances, which usually depend on a specific act of the subject, may necessitate a change from a loose surveillance to a close surveillance. Preplanning is of assistance, but the investigator must observe and interpret the act or circumstances properly and accurately in order to implement the plan. If an overall plan is for a loose surveillance until the completion of an act, or the meeting of a person, after which the subject is to be kept under close surveillance or apprehended, a proper determination must be made as to when the specific incident has taken place.

Techniques of Foot Surveillance

One-man Surveillance. A one-man surveillance is best employed in a situation calling for a fixed surveillance. It should be avoided in a moving surveillance because it does not provide for flexibility. If a moving one-man surveillance must be resorted to, the surveillant should operate to the rear of the subject when on the same side of the street and keep as close as possible to the subject in order to observe his actions and to make successful apprehension at the appropriate time. Crowd and street conditions will dictate the appropriate distance to be maintained between the subject and surveillant. When the subject turns a corner in an uncrowded area the surveillant should continue crossing across the intersecting street. By glancing up the street in the direction the subject traveled, he can note the subject's position and actions, and act accordingly. The surveillant can operate from across the street from the subject and recross the street at his leisure to fall in behind the subject.

In a crowded area the surveillant should decrease the distance between himself and the subject, and observe the subject from the corner. Unless the subject is standing just around the corner, the surveillance can be continued from the same side of the street. Do not turn a corner immediately behind the subject. When operating across the street from the subject, circumstances will dictate whether to operate forward, to the rear, or abreast of the subject. The surveillant should be abreast of the subject when he turns a corner to enable the observation of any contact made or entries into buildings.

If the subject enters a railroad station or a bus depot ticket line, the surveillant should endeavor to get right behind him to learn his destination or overhear his conversation with the clerk. If the subject enters a telephone booth, the surveillant should enter an adjacent one to overhear any conversation, if possible. The subject may be simulating making a telephone call to see if he is being followed. An effort should be made to recover items discarded by the subject or to recover second sheets from pads which the subject has used. However, the surveillant should avoid picking up an item discarded by the subject when this might lead to recognition of the surveillant.

Two-Man or "AB" Surveillance. In the "AB" technique of surveillance, the surveillant directly behind the subject is known as the "A" surveillant. "A" follows the subject, and "B" follows "A" either on the same side of the street or from across the street. When both surveillants operate on the same side of the street as the subject, and the subject turns a corner, "A" continues in the original direction and crosses the intersecting street, and from a vantage point there signals the correct moves to "B." "B" should not turn the corner or come into sight until he has received the signal. When "B" is operating across the street and the subject turns a corner to the right, away from "B", "B" will cross the street behind the subject and take up the "A" position. This move should be pre-arranged, and no signals should be necessary. All visual signals employed should be discreet and consistent with the environment (see Figure 1).

Should the subject turn to the left and cross the street toward "B," "B" should drop back to avoid meeting the subject. "B" could go into a store, or continue straight ahead. "B" should keep "A" in sight to observe his signals indicating what the next move should be (see Figure 2).

Three-Man or "ABC" Surveillance. The "ABC" technique of surveillance is intended to keep two sides of the subject covered. "A" follows the subject. "B" follows "A" and concentrates on keeping "A" in sight rather than the subject. The normal position for "B" is behind "A." "C" normally operates across the street from the subject and

7

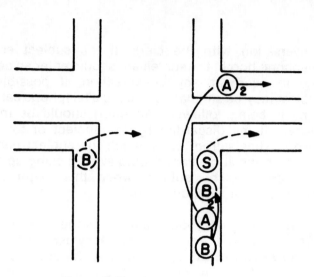

Figure 1. Turning corner to right.

Ⓢ **SUBJECT**

◌ **ALTERNATE POSITIONS**

○ **SUBSCRIPTS INDICATE FIRST AND**
SUBSEQUENT POSITIONS

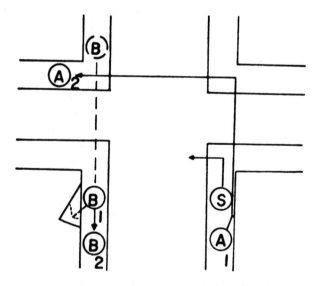

Figure 2. Turning corner to left.

8

slightly to his rear, enabling "C" to observe the subject without turning his head. Variations such as having both "B" and "C" across the street or all three of the surveillants behind the subject on the same side of the street may be necessary due to crowded conditions or vehicular traffic. In this technique, if the subject turns a corner, "A" continues in the original direction, crosses the intersecting street, and signals instructions to the other surveillants from that vantage point. Either "B" or "C" can be given the "A" position and "A" may take up the original "C" position and continue his observation of the subject from across the street (see Figure 3).

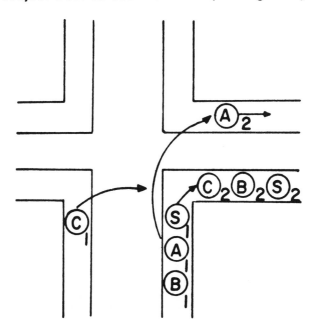

Figure 3. Variation of the "ABC" technique.

Ⓢ SUBJECT

◌ ALTERNATE POSITIONS

$\underset{\text{I}}{\text{O}}$ SUBSCRIPTS INDICATE FIRST AND SUBSEQUENT POSITIONS

In another variation of this technique, both "A" and "B" may continue in the original direction and cross the street. "A" signals "C" to take up the "A" position. "B" then recrosses the street and assumes his former "B" position. "A" assumes the "C" position (see Figure 4). In the third situation, when "C" notices that the subject is about to turn a corner, he signals both "A" and "B" what positions to assume.

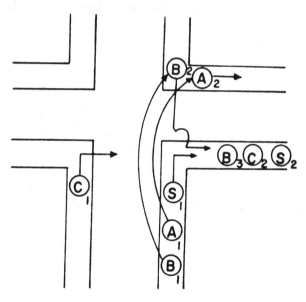

Figure 4. Another variation of the "ABC" technique.

Ⓢ **SUBJECT**

◌ **ALTERNATE POSITIONS**

Q **SUBSCRIPTS INDICATE FIRST AND SUBSEQUENT POSITIONS**

Other Techniques. Other techniques are resorted to in order to lessen the chance of a surveillant being "made." One such technique is that, by either prearrangement or signal, the two or more surveillants will change places with each other. This technique is commonly referred to as the leap-frog method. Progressive surveillance is another technique used when extreme caution is mandatory. In situations where it is presupposed that the subject will use all possible methods to elude surveillants this technique may be used. It is a slow method and is limited to situations where there is plenty of time and to subjects who follow habitual daily routines. When this technique is adopted, the subject is followed a certain distance and the surveillance is discontinued and the time noted. The next day another surveillant picks up the subject at the time and place where the surveillance was previously discontinued, and again follows the subject for a short distance. This continues day after day until the surveillance is completed or discontinued.

Techniques of Vehicle Surveillance

General. A vehicle is necessary when the subject is moving around in an automobile. This type of surveillance demands additional preparations to those used for a foot surveillance. A dependable vehicle must be provided similar to types commonly used in the area in which the surveillance is to take place. This may be a panel truck, automobile or large truck or trailer. The license plates on the surveillant's vehicle must not be identifiable as being official. They should be of the state or country in which the surveillance will take place. If more than one vehicle is to be used, two-way radio is advantageous. Consideration should be given to the possible necessity of providing for additional gasoline, water, first aid equipment and roadmaps.

Two surveillants must be provided for vehicle surveillance. It is advantageous to combine foot and vehicular surveillance whenever possible. The surveillants will remain more alert, it will forestall boredom, and prevent an apathetic surveillance. When a subject turns a corner,

11

if one surveillant dismounts, he can better observe the subject's actions and signal his partner to make appropriate moves. When a subject parks his vehicle and remains in it, a surveillant on foot can better observe the subject's actions and those of passers-by. An accomplice of the subject could easily throw, or drop, some object into the car without being seen if both surveillants remain in their car.

As in foot surveillance, vehicular surveillance requires inconspicuous actions. The surveillants should stay in the same lane as the subject to avoid having to make turns from the wrong lane. If the situation permits, the surveillants should change direction, such as going around a block, to break continuity before the suspect becomes suspicious. It is much more difficult for the surveillants at night to be sure that they are following the right vehicle. The subject's car can be better kept in sight if the car is distinctive. If the opportunity presents itself, a piece of reflectorized tape may be attached to the rear of the car or a red tail-light glass can be broken. A white rear light is easily followed. The surveillant's car should also receive such attention. The dome light should be disconnected so that the light will not show when a door is opened. One of the headlights and the license plate light can be wired to permit them to be turned on or off independently. This will permit a change in the traffic pattern as seen by the subject.

One-Vehicle Surveillance. When one vehicle is used for surveillance it must remain close enough behind the subject to permit the surveillants to observe his actions, but far enough behind to escape detection. When a subject's car stops, one surveillant should follow his actions on foot. The subject will not expect to be tailed by a person on foot while he is using his vehicle. When the subject turns a corner, the surveillants may make one of two possible moves. They may continue in the original direction, cross the intersecting street and make a U-turn; the subject will take little interest in a car turning into the street behind him coming from a direction that is opposite to that which he was traveling before turning the corner. An alternate move would be to continue in the original direction, crossing the intersecting street and continuing around the block. The subject will not expect to be tailed by a car approaching him from a direction to his front.

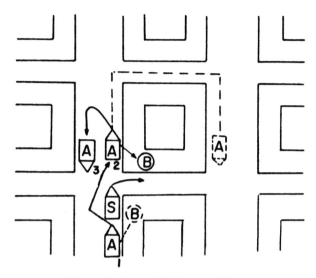

Figure 5. One-vehicle surveillance.

⌂ **SUBJECT**

⌂ **SURVEILLANTS**

Ⓑ **SURVEILLANT ON FOOT**

○⌂ **ALTERNATE POSITIONS**

SUBSCRIPTS INDICATE FIRST AND SUBSEQUENT POSITIONS

Two-Vehicle Surveillance. This technique employs two vehicles to follow the subject at different distances on the same street, as in the "AB" method of foot surveillance. This technique can be varied by having one vehicle going in the same direction as the subject on a parallel street while receiving radio-transmitted directions from the surveillants directly behind the subject. This technique is more flexible than the one-vehicle surveillance in that two vehicles can exchange places from time to time, or one vehicle can precede the subject. If more vehicles and people are available, other techniques can be planned that are even more flexible.

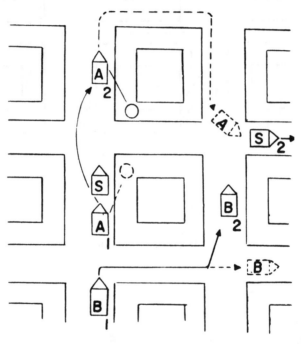

Figure 6. Two-vehicle surveillance

|S| **SUBJECT**

|A| **SURVEILLANTS**

(B) **SURVEILLANT ON FOOT**

ALTERNATE POSITIONS

SUBSCRIPTS INDICATE FIRST AND SUBSEQUENT POSITIONS

Fixed Surveillance

In a fixed surveillance, or stakeout, it is the subject that remains stationary. The surveillant may move around for closer observation of the area or subject. When one surveillant is detailed to watch a place with more than one exit, the surveillant may have to move about considerably in order to maintain the proper surveillance. When preparing for a stakeout, the base of operations should be well planned. It may be a store, apartment, house, automobile or truck. A thorough, but cautious, reconnaissance should be conducted of the area or building from which the surveillance is to be made. Necessary equipment such as binoculars, electronic investigative aids, cameras and sound recording devices should be provided. Specific arrangements should be made to provide relief for the surveillants and for communications contact with headquarters.

In situations in which the surveillant can not observe from a fixed base it may be necessary for him to assume a role such as a salesman, junk collector, telephone repairman, newspaper vendor or other occupation that will not attract undue attention. The use of disguised vans and trucks as observation posts in fixed surveillances should be considered.

UNDERCOVER INVESTIGATIONS

General

An investigator is undercover when he officially abandons his identity as an investigator and adopts an identity which is calculated to enable him to associate with, and get information frcm, one or more persons without their knowing his true identity. The degree to which a false identity is assumed is dependent upon the incident under investigation. The assumed identity may merely involve the adoption of an assumed name, or it may require elaborate preparation. Whatever the preparation is, it should be aimed at precluding compromise, avoiding danger to the investigator and insuring ultimate success of the investigation.

Normally an undercover investigation should not be attempted until all other investigative techniques have failed, or are deemed impractical.

The following are factors which should be considered before an undercover investigation is started: • the results desired • the importance of the investigation • available planning information • availability of qualified personnel • the amounts and kinds of equipment needed • and the degree of the potential danger to the investigator.

Qualifications for Assignment

General. Experience has demonstrated the usefulness of undercover work as a means of securing valuable evidence. It has also demonstrated that not every man is adaptable to this type of work. An investigator who will be assigned to undercover work should be well trained and experienced. He should be a resourceful individual possessing good judgement and complete self-confidence. He must be physically strong and possess courage to meet unforseen situations. He must be able to make quick and sound decisions.

Special. In addition to the general qualifications, an investigator should have the ability to act in a particular assumed role. He must have a memory capable of recalling incidents without the use of notes. In many undercover assignments notes can not be taken, and reports can not be sent to headquarters. If an occupation is assumed, he must be skilled in that occupation. His physical appearance and capabilities must be consistent with his qualifications. He must be well grounded in the terminology and techniques of the subject's professional operations. In some situations, the undercover investigator must also have a linguistic ability. Other deciding factors to be taken into consideration in the selection of the investigator may include his hobbies, interest in sports, musical ability or his professional background.

Preparation and Planning

Continuous effort must be made to obtain and develop all available information concerning the subjects and their connection with the known or suspected crime. Such information may include: location of outlets for stolen contraband goods; subjects' methods of operation; detailed personal data on all subjects; and any information which may contribute to the successful undercover mission. This information should be developed with care to avoid alerting the subjects or their associates. Only those persons should be informed of the contemplated undercover investigation whose knowledge thereof will distinctly contribute to the ultimate success of the investigation.

In order to conceal the true identity of the investigator, a background or cover story must be constructed. It should be built to help the investigator gain the confidence of the subject and should seldom, if ever, be wholly fictitious. Every practical effort should be made to have the story conform to the actual history of the investigator. The investigator should purport to be from a city with which he is familiar, but not in the area in which the home city of the subject is located. Arrangements should be made to have key principals in the fictitious history corroborate the assertions of the undercover investigator.

Personal possessions must be appropriate to the assumed character in quality, price, age, fit and degree of cleanliness. All clothing should have laundry marks consistant with the story. The investigator should study and emulate the mannerisms, gestures and speech of those with whom he will associate. He should also discover their likes and tastes in food and music. He must be prepared to work late hours and be in constant personal danger.

Particular attention should be paid to various items carried by the undercover investigator such as pocketbooks, watches, rings, tokens, suitcases, ticket stubs, miscellaneous papers, brand of tobacco, matches, letters, sums of money and other personal items. Documents or identity cards should show the appropriate amount of wear. The investigator should be able to explain naturally and logically how each item came into his possession. A weapon should be carried only if it is in keeping with the background story.

Pretend infirmities are dangerous. They are difficult to maintain for any length of time and may give the investigator away in time of stress. Only when absolutely necessary should any infirmity be adopted. Employment of female counterparts to create the impression of a couple is advisable to allay any compromise which might be brought about by the singular presence of an undercover investigator.

In certain undercover situations, names, addresses and numbers may be disguised in the form of telephone numbers, bets or similar harmless writings. Communications with headquarters or the controlling investigator may be through disguised or concealed letter drops, or conducted through intermediaries of established reliability.

Some method of communication should be devised so that the undercover investigator can communicate with headquarters. The method should be simple and practical. Signals may be arranged with an investigator who is keeping the undercover investigator under surveillance. A telephone call can usually be made from a public telephone under a reasonable pretext. Extreme care should be exercised if written messages are to be used.

Part of the planning should provide for a natural contact between the undercover investigator and the subject. In addition to providing for the investigator to be placed in the locality or unit with the subject, the background story should contain elements which will induce a meeting without apparent effort on the part of the investigator. A mutual interest in hobbies, athletic contests and other leisure time activities provide a medium for getting acquainted. The investigator should not pose as an authority on a subject unless he is well qualified. Many times an admitted lack of knowledge, but an interest in, a given subject will cause an advance by the subject so he can display his knowledge. Unless it is absolutely necessary the investigator should not pose as a criminal.

NIGHT SURVEILLANCE EQUIPMENT FOR LAW ENFORCEMENT

TYPES OF NIGHT VIEWING DEVICES

Basically, there are two types of Night Viewing Devices: active and passive. The active type puts out its own light source, an infrared beam, which is visable to the user through the infrared scope which is part of the unit. The advantage of the active type of night viewing device is that the user can see in *total* darkness, since he does not have to depend on available light from the environment. Disadvantages of the active night viewers are limited range, and the fact that the infrared beam is visible to anyone else looking through an infrared scope, or through a passive night viewing device.

The passive type of night viewing device electronically amplifies whatever existing light is in the environment, such as moonlight, starlight, or sky glow, which is why such units are sometimes referred to as "starlight scopes."

Night Viewing Devices have been developed for use by law enforcement agencies since 1969. This includes small city departments and larger, more sophisticated police departments, government agencies, State and County sheriffs departments.

The purpose of this chapter is to acquaint the reader with various types of Night Viewing Devices available, and to aid in the selection of an NVD and its accessories.

USE OF NVD'S AND ACCESSORIES

The FBI reports that the majority of crimes are committed at night under the cloak of darkness. Most riots and student demonstrations also occur at night for the simple reason that it is more difficult for the police officers to obtain evidence that will hold up in court. The

1968 Democratic Convention in Chicago is a perfect example.

The primary purpose of Night Viewing Devices is to permit police officers to carefully observe events occurring over one block away at night.

These Night Viewing Devices, with adaptors, can be attached to the front of cameras to provide a means of obtaining evidence that has been proven to stand up in court. Television-video tapes, movies, and still photos can all be obtained using Night Viewing Devices.

THEORY OF OPERATION:
FIRST AND SECOND GENERATION NVD'S

Two basic types of passive Night Viewing Devices are marketed. They are called first and second generation units. A brief explanation of the image intensifier tube theory of operation will aid the potential user of NVD equipment in the selection of a unit to satisfy his requirements.

First Generation - Image Intensifiers

The first image intensifiers developed are classified as first generation tubes. They operate in the following way as graphically shown in Diagram 1.

Technical Explanation of First Generation Intensifiers

Particles of light called photons pass through the lens and impinge on the photocathode. of the intensifier (Diagram 1). After several photons strike an area of the photocathode, an electron is knocked loose. 12,000 volts of electricity captures the electron and greatly accelerates it in the desired direction. The electron, traveling at a tremendous velocity, smashes into a phosphor screen at the opposite end of the tube, creating a glow where it strikes. This light is about 40 times brighter than the original level striking the photocathode.

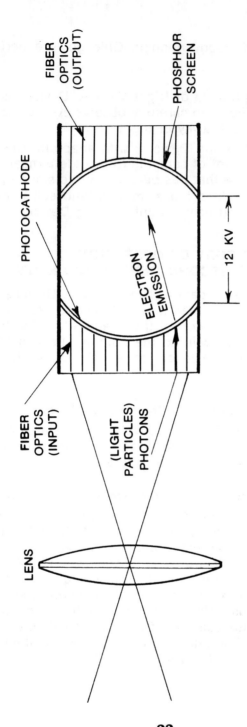

Diagram 1. First Generation Image Intensifier Operation.

LENS

FIBER OPTICS (INPUT)

(LIGHT PARTICLES) PHOTONS

PHOTOCATHODE

ELECTRON EMISSION

12 KV

FIBER OPTICS (OUTPUT)

PHOSPHOR SCREEN

22

It is possible to bond image intensifiers together and further increase the amplification. In other words, two intensifiers in series would amplify light 40 x 40 or 1600 times, and three intensifiers would increase the level 40 x 40 x 40 or 64,000 times.

Advantages and Disadvantages
of First Generation Intensifiers

First generation Night Viewing Devices use three first generation image intensifiers bonded together into one unit as shown in Diagram 2. These tubes were used in Vietnam in the original U.S. Army Starlight Scope.

The intensifiers are of proven quality, rugged and have excellent resolution (approx. 40 lp/mm). They can withstand a 75 g shock which is substantial. However, the military, for whom the device was originally developed, felt the unit was too large for their personnel. This led to the development of the smaller second generation NVD's. Another minor fault of the first generation tubes was the introduction of a large amount of distortion on the edges of the scene which is apparent in photographs taken through an NVD.

Second Generation Image Intensifiers

The design of the second generation image intensifiers was intitiated to reduce its size and weight and to improve on the first generation units. However, this effort was only partially successful.

Technical Explanations
of Second Generation Intensifiers

Engineers learned that by introducing a small disc called a micro-channel plate (MCP) into an intensifier as depicted in Diagram 3, they could enhance the sensitivity or gain.

These intensifiers function exactly like the first generation units, except that when an electron strikes the microchannel plate, it dislodges and drives a large

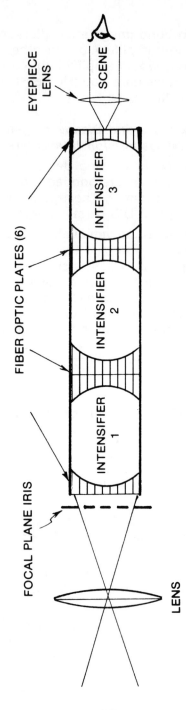

EYEPIECE LENS

SCENE

FIBER OPTIC PLATES (6)

INTENSIFIER 3

INTENSIFIER 2

INTENSIFIER 1

FOCAL PLANE IRIS

LENS

Diagram 2. First Generation Night Viewing Devices — Three Stages Bonded Together.

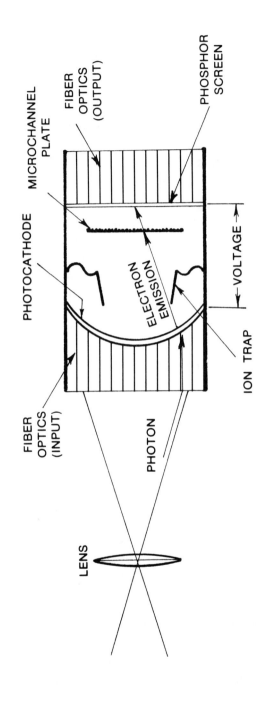

Diagram 3. Second Generation Image Intensifier Operation.

LENS

FIBER OPTICS (INPUT)

PHOTON

PHOTOCATHODE

ELECTRON EMISSION

MICROCHANNEL PLATE

FIBER OPTICS (OUTPUT)

PHOSPHOR SCREEN

VOLTAGE

ION TRAP

quantity of electrons obtaining a gain equal to three first generation intensifiers bonded together. In addition, the distortion introduced by these units is approximately 1/5 that of earlier intensifiers.

Advantages and Disadvantages
of Second Generation Intensifiers

While the physical size of the intensifier and the amount of distortion introduced by the tube were both reduced, some disadvantages also resulted. The resolution of second generation intensifiers is less than the older units, and the cost of manufacturing these devices is considerably higher than previous units.

Second generation units have been perfected sufficiently that the military is using them to replace first generation units. They also have been ruggedized to the degree that they can withstand a 75 g shock (gun mounts).

BUYER PROTECTION INFORMATION

A buyer must be knowledgeable about Night Viewing Devices prior to purchasing because of both the high cost of the equipment, and the inferior quality of some available models.

Basic Price

Some NVD's are listed at a low price with specifications making them appear to be comparable to "higher" cost units.

However, added features cost extra, and ultimately you actually pay more. Some questions you must ask are: "Exactly what are these features?" "Are they required?" "Are they included in the price?"

Automatic Brightness Control (ABC)

A Night Viewing Device amplifies available light sufficiently to provide a good view to the observer. Any gain over the threshold limit tends to burn the device out or reduce its life. The ABC is designed to automatically adjust and maintain the gain at a correct operation level. If a bright light is directed toward the viewer, the ABC reduces the gain to a safe level. If the observer looks from an area illuminated by a street light to a very dark area, the ABC automatically increases the gain.

This feature frees the observer from being required to make adjustments and also protects the unit. This feature is mandatory for police work, especially since many of the officers using the equipment may be briefly trained. The officer is free to do his job, which is to observe, and not to make adjustments.

Some manufacturers do not include this feature in their equipment or they charge extra for it.

Focal Plane Iris

A focal plane iris is a separate iris from the object lens and is located on the front of the viewer behind the lens. It permits an officer to do several things:

- He can close it down and reduce the size of the field of view.
- He can block out bright lights on the edge of the scene, protecting the intensifier.
- When an automobile is being driven away from the observer, the tail lights appear as large bright areas in the scene and the license number can not be obtained. By closing down the focal plane iris, the observer can blot out the tail lights, enabling the license number to be read.
- In a scene where there are many bright lights, details can be observed using the iris that are impossible to detect without it.
- Closing down the iris enables the officer to look into a darkened area surrounded by bright lights. This feature permits the officer to see areas that viewers without this feature could not observe. Many manufacturers do not offer this feature in their NVD's. It is our experience that urban and suburban operation requires a focal plane iris.

27

Closed Eye Guard

Night Viewing Devices emit a yellow-green light from the phosphor screen. This light passes through the eyepiece lens into the eye of the observer, enabling him to see. However, when the observer removes or lowers the viewer from his eye, the light emitted illuminates the observer's face. This makes him detectable by the person being observed. This is very undesireable, especially when the viewer is being used to locate snipers or armed criminals.

The Army Starlight scope uses an eyeguard that snaps shut when removed from the observer's eye, preventing light from escaping and making it safe to use under all conditions.

Specifications: Be Aware and Beware

Minimum Performance Specs

Specifications are printed by manufacturers to guarantee their products' performance to the buyer. As an example, the main purpose of a Night Viewing Device is to amplify light, a parameter which is specified as luminance gain. If a manufacturer specifies a minimum gain of 30,000, then a large number of his units perform very near that level or he would raise the minimum guarantee. Some manufacturers hide their low guarantees by stating average or typical values much higher than their minimum figure. They then point out to the buyer, "Look, we offer an average gain of 50,000."

These average or typical specifications are worthless and guarantee nothing to the buyer. The only parameter guaranteeing the buyer a specified gain is the minimum specification.

Weight

Weight is one of the most important parameters to the police officer in selecting an NVD. It is desireable to purchase the lightest unit because after the officer carries or holds the viewer to his eye for a period of time, each additional ounce feels like an extra pound. Yet some suppliers manufacture identically performing units weighing two to three pounds more.

It is also common to present weight specifications by specifying the unit weight, omitting the objective lens which can be as much as five pounds.

Accessories

Many police departments purchase Night Viewing Devices, and obtain excellent results until they decide to buy additional accessories such as a photographic adaptor.

To their dismay, they learn that the cost of this adaptor is almost half the price of the original device. They are forced to buy the adapter from the viewer manufacturer, because other less expensive adaptors are not compatible to his unit. This technique enables manufacturers to sell viewers at reduced costs and then make up the difference on the high cost of accessories.

Equally important, it is desireable to learn if all the required accessories are offered by the manufacture prior to purchasing a viewer. Most manufacturers offer a limited number of accessories. The buyer could purchase an expensive viewer with limited capacity, resulting in the necessity to purchase a new viewer from a different source, or having to tolerate limited viewing capacities.

Photographic Camera Adaptors

Some viewers can only be used with one type of camera, e.g., a Cannon. If a police photography laboratory has a different type in inventory, they may be required to purchase new cameras to operate with the viewer, creating an added expense.

Other manufacturers offer special light meters to go with their cameras at additional cost. Caution is advised because an observer has to take a reading through the light meter, turn on a flashlight to see to adjust the camera, make the adjustments, turn off the flashlight and

Normal City Illumination (2×10^3 ft-C)

	Object	Various Lenses		
		75mm lens f/1.4	135mm lens f/1.8	300mm lens f/3.2
Notes	6-foot man			
(1)	Able to observe	500 feet	900 feet	1300 feet
(2)	Close Inspection	300 feet	540 feet	780 feet
(3)	Read License Plates	90 feet	190 feet	300 feet

NOTES

1. "Able to observe" means that the sex of a person can be determined as well as what the person is doing.

2. "Close Inspection" means details are observable such as facial features and articles of clothing.

3. "Read License Plates" — data was obtained using parked cars in between street lights or at the darkest part of a normal city street. The car lights were not on, since an illuminated license plate can be observed much further.

Diagram 4. Night Viewing Device Range Guide; Target Reflection = 10%.

then snap the photograph. It is not believed that many police officers would desire to give away their position by turning on a light to go through this procedure.

LENS INTERCHANGEABILITY: RANGE/DISTANCE

This is one of the more important features of any Night Viewing Device. Most police departments already have a supply of lenses available, making it desireable to select a viewer which is compatible to the inventory. This is very important, since lenses are expensive.

How Far Can You See?

One of the most frequently asked questions is, "How far can you see with an NVD?" Night Viewing Devices can see to the horizon; they are not limited to short distances like old Infrared units. The distance at which an object can be recognized is dependent on a number of factors, principaly the focal length and the f# of the lens. As the focal length of the lens increases, so does the magnification of the target. The lower the f#, the more light passes through the lens resulting in a clearer image.

As a rule of thumb, the following guide is provided to show the distance at which objects can be observed at normal city light illumination levels.

ELECTRONIC EAVESDROPPING TECHNIQUES AND EQUIPMENT

INTRODUCTION

Voice surveillance using electronic techniques has become an essential activity of law enforcement organizations at almost all levels of government. Often the lives and safety of law enforcement officers, and others as well, depend upon the reliability of miniaturized and concealed communications devices. Furthermore, apprehension of criminals and the successful prosecution of criminal cases can depend upon evidence obtained by these techniques. These considerations clearly indicate the importance of this type of equipment.

This chapter has a two-fold purpose: first, to help inform law enforcement personnel concerning the application and functioning of undercover *communications equipment* and, second, to set standards to be used in the selection, evaluation and procurement of such equipment.

The information contained in this chapter has been derived from a number of sources, including law enforcement personnel, manufacturers, publications and laboratory measurements. This chapter is concerned with the types of devices available and their application, capabilities, advantages and disadvantages. An attempt has been made to bring together a body of information which will assist the police officer in performing his duties safely and effectively. Although the variety of circumstances under which such equipment may be used is seemingly unlimited, there are some basic technical rules, facts and techniques which are generally applicable in most situations. Understanding and using scientific techniques can go a long way toward the realization of success in an undercover surveillance situation.

While the topic of immediate interest is surveillance or offensive activity, counter-surveillance or defensive activity cannot be ignored completely because of the strong influence these activities have on each other. Being involved with either of these activities requires a sound knowledge of the other. While a detailed treatment of countersurveillance is not within the scope of this chapter, it will be mentioned where it is of importance in the understanding of surveillance equipment and its use.

The equipment and techniques discussed herein are concerned only with the interception of voice or audio communication, and, therefore, no information is included on video or optical techniques.

RADIATING DEVICES AND RECEIVERS

General

In this catagory is the miniaturized transmitter which may be worn on the body, concealed in some stationary location, or concealed in a vehicle or portable container of almost any type. Because of this versatility, the miniature transmitter is used in a wide variety of situations. These transmitters are particularly useful in circumstances where unrestricted mobility is required. In contrast to hard-wire devices (covered later in this chapter), the miniature transmitter is most often used when operation is required for only a relatively short period of time, such as a few minutes or hours rather than days or weeks. This time limitation is imposed primarily by the lifetime of the power supply.

The use of miniature transmitters brings into play a great many factors which can cause performance to vary widely in seemingly similar circumstances. In this context, it is useful to look at a complete communications system involving the transmitter, the propagation medium and the receiver. Figure 1 is highly oversimplified; relaying information successfully from one location to another is an involved procedure. It has been estimated by users of typical equipment that the causes of failure are approximately as follows:

Percent

Power supply failure (batteries) 50
Operator Error 45
Equipment Failure (circuitry) 5

Because surveillance needs often arise on short notice and adverse conditions are frequently encountered, it is imperative that persons using surveillance equipment become familiar with all aspects of its use. The importance of well-trained personnel can hardly be overemphasized.

Operating Frequencies

With few exceptions, miniature transmitters used in police work operate in the following four frequency ranges:

25-80 MHz
88-120 MHz
150-174 MHz
400-512 MHz

Some experimental work has been conducted over the past few decades to determine which frequencies are best from a propagation standpoint, but the investigators have not produced conclusive evidence indicating that one frequency is better that another in a majority of circumstances. One such investigation compared propagation into buildings at 35 MHz with that at 150 MHz. In this study, 150 MHz was found to be slightly better on a statistical basis, but the difference was so small that the issue must still remain in doubt as far as any specific situation is concerned. Other work was reported regarding the propagation behavior of frequencies from 0.1 to 1.0 GHz as related to communication from the inside of automobiles. The study clearly showed some frequencies to be superior than others, but factors other than frequency influenced the measurements so that definite conclusions concerning frequency selection could not be drawn.

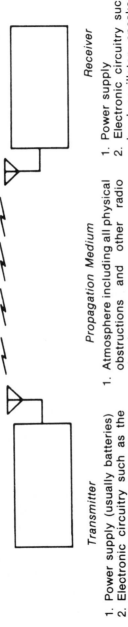

Transmitter
1. Power supply (usually batteries)
2. Electronic circuitry such as the oscillator, modulator, amplifiers, and filters
3. Antenna

Propagation Medium
1. Atmosphere including all physical obstructions and other radio signals

Receiver
1. Power supply
2. Electronic circuitry such as the local oscillator, speaker, amplifiers and speakers
3. Antenna

Figure 1. Model communication system.

35

For a number of reasons, the trend has been toward the higher frequencies. The use of higher frequencies is advantageous because shorter antennas are easier to conceal. Figure 2 shows the length of quarter-wavelength antennas in air for frequencies in the range of 25 to 600 MHz, with the specific frequency bands mentioned above shown as the solid portions of the curve. Note that at 25 MHz a quarter-wavelength antenna would be 300 centimeters (approximately 10 feet) long, while at 500 MHz it is only 15 centimeters (approximately ½ foot) long. The use of antennas shorter than a quarter-wavelength reduces radiation efficiency, thus reducing effective communication range.

Interference must also be taken into consideration in frequency selection. Both man-made and natural interference decrease significantly with increasing frequency, which further strengthens the tendency toward the use of higher frequencies. As more use has been made of radios for communications purposes, the lower frequency bands have been more crowded, constantly increasing the chances for interference or interception. As a precaution, an FM receiver can be used to monitor the frequency spectrum in the location where the undercover operation is to take place, and an unused frequency can be selected.

The use of higher frequencies improves the signal-to-noise ratio. As solid state technology improves and better devices and techniques are developed, the use of frequencies above the UHF region will almost certainly become common practice for surveillance work.

25-50 MHz Band

The use of frequencies in this band for surveillance purposes is decreasing. There are several reasons for this. Principally, this band offers poor security compared to higher frequency bands. The 25 to 50 MHz band is very heavily used, and this has greatly increased the possibility of either undesired detection or interference from other signal sources. In addition, these frequencies are reflected by the night-time ionosphere, further increasing the problems of interference and security.

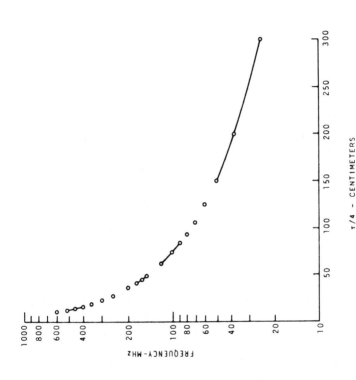

Figure 2. Length (in air) of quarter-wavelength antennas for the frequency range from 25 to 600 MHz.

37

These disadvantages, coupled with the requirement for fairly long antennas which are difficult to conceal, have caused surveillance personnel to abandon these frequencies for higher ones.

Harmonic radiation is an additional disadvantage of operation in the 25-50 MHz band. Transistor oscillators are characteristically rich in odd-number harmonics, and unless output is filtered, their use can lead to difficulties for other users. The third harmonics of frequencies between 29.3 to 40 MHz fall within the 88 to 120 MHz band. Unfiltered transmissions can thus result in detection by receivers operating in the 88 to 108 MHz commercial FM band or interference with aircraft communication.

88-120 MHz Band

This frequency range includes the commercial broadcast FM band extending from 88 to 108 MHz. Receivers of good quality are mass produced and may be purchased at prices far below those of receivers of comparable quality on other frequency bands. Also, some of those receivers can be tuned to operate above the commercial FM band, at frequencies as high as 120 MHz. For these reasons, the 88 to 120 MHz frequency range is attractive, and has been widely used for surveillance purposes.

There are several reasons, however, why such use is undesireable. With millions of receivers in this band in constant use, it is evident that this frequency range affords less security than almost any frequency band that could be chosen. Also of importance is the fact that the commonly available commercial receiver is not crystal controlled and, therefore, more subject to drift with the attendant loss of signal strength. A second reason for avoiding this frequency band is that the portion from 108 to 120 MHz is used for aircraft landing systems, and any interference, especially in the vicinity of airports, can be very dangerous. Some electronic eavesdropping equipment manufacturers produce and sell equipment which operates at these frequencies, and articles have been written which openly advocate use of the aircraft band. While there may be no intention to create a hazard, it is evident that once a device is sold, the manufacturer loses all control over its use. The best policy is not to use equipment operating in this range. It is not only a potential hazard, but is also in violation of FCC and FAA regulations.

150-174 MHz Band

Surveillance equipment using these frequencies is usually more sophisticated in design than that designed to operate at lower frequencies. Most of the higher quality body-mounted transmitters and receivers manufactured during the past few years operate within this band. When comparing this frequency range with the lower ones already discussed, several advantages appear. First, better security exists because there are fewer receivers in existence. Next, interference is lower because of lighter communication traffic, lower incidence of ionosphere reflection, and lower levels of natural and man-made noise. Finally, higher radiation efficiencies can be achieved using shorter antennas.

400-512 MHz Band

Even lower interference is likely in this band and detectors which might lead to discovery are relatively rare. However, some reception difficulties can be expected in areas where physical obstructions are numerous. The shorter antennas required may be an overriding consideration because, at these frequencies, a quarter-wavelength antenna can be easily concealed.

Summary

Following is a summary of the significant points regarding the four frequency ranges:

	Advantages	Disadvantages
25 to 50 MHz	a. For same power, possibly better coverage in crowded areas.	a. Requires longer antennas. b. A much-used frequency band, with consequently poor security. c. Skywave propagation at night may result in undesired signal transmission or reception. d. Third harmonic radiation.
88 to 120 MHz	a. Low cost receivers available.	a. Violates FCC regulation. b. Minimum security; easily monitored because of availability of receivers. c. 108 to 120 MHz may interfere with aircraft navigation and communication.
150 to 174 MHz	a. Quarter-wavelength antennas short enough for concealment on body. b. Good equipment available. c. Good security compared to lower frequencies.	a. Equipment is expensive. b. Band heavily used in many areas of the country.
400 to 512 MHz	a. Rarely monitored; best from security standpoint. b. Requires very short antennas. c. Low level of interference.	a. Equipment is expensive. b. Few sources of equipment.

Power Ouput, Operating Time and Operating Distance

The maximum practical distance between transmitter and receiver for satisfactory communication can be very important in surveillance applications. This distance is dependent upon a number of things, including transmitter power output, gains of transmitting and receiving antennas, and receiver sensitivity. Still other factors are the local conditions, such as the terrain, the conductivity and dielectric constant of the earth, the building density, and the heights of antennas. The fact that any or all of these factors may vary with time and location makes accurate prediction of operating distance nearly impossible. General statements are often made about the operating distance or coverage area of a transmitter, but it is unwise to rely heavily upon information of this type. Such statements are likely to be based on a few specific experiences in a given locality, and performance may be found to differ widely in different situations. Claims about operating distance are not dependable criteria for determining the effectiveness of a transmitter under a given set of conditions and should not be used to determine the superiority of one transmitter over another.

There are two approaches to objective measurement of transmitter output. One is to make comparative field strength measurements under carefully standardized conditions, and the other is to measure the transmitter power into a 50-ohm termination. Either approach may present difficulties. The field strength approach requires a measurement site free of obstruction and a receiver or field strength meter. The intensity of the field radiated by each transmitter must be measured and plotted over a period of time. This method presents several problems, including the determination of the proper type of antenna to use to achieve accurate data, the necessity for receiver calibration in the case where the transmitters to be compared operate on different frequencies, and the possibility of other radio signals on the same frequency leading to erroneous field strength measurements. Clearly, this is not an ideal approach unless field test facilities and highly skilled personnel are available.

Using the power output measurement approach is much simpler, but not without possible complications. The procedure is to connect a good quality power meter to the antenna output terminal of the transmitter and record the power over a specified time interval. However, power meters do not yield accurate results unless the output impedance of the transmitter matches the input impedance of the power meter. The input impedance of most power meters is 50 ohms. Providing the output impedance of the transmitter is also 50 ohms, an adapter from the transmitter output connector to the power meter input connector is usually all that is needed to make the measurement. If the output impedance of the transmitter is not 50 ohms, some sort of a matching or tuning network is necessary. The tuning network is inserted between the transmitter and power meter and is varied until the power meter reading is maximized, after which the measurement can proceed.

It is common to encounter miniature surveillance transmitters which are neither 50 ohms at the antenna output connector nor equipped with a coaxial connector. Some do not have a ground connection but instead have only a screw terminal for the attachment of an antenna wire. With such a combination of output connectors and terminal conditions, the task of making meaningful measurements becomes extremely difficult.

There is a need for standardization if there is to be meaningful and objective comparison of equipment performance. Ideally, there should be a convenient and straightforward means of measuring transmitter power output without ambiguity, and specifications should spell out not only maximum transmitter power output but also some indication of how this power decreases with transmission time.

One final, important point regarding the measurement of transmitter power output using a power meter is the manner in which the power is distributed over the frequency spectrum. Because most power meters use a broadband resistive element, such as a bolometer, as the sensing device, the power measurement alone will not provide sufficient information. If a particular transmitter has an output spectrum rich in harmonics, it will not be distinguishable from a second transmitter which shows the same power output but has had the harmonic frequencies drastically suppressed. It is possible to have a situation where as much as one-half of the power radiated is at the harmonic and other suppressed frequencies. Such spurious radiation is detrimental in that it substantially increases the risk of detection.

Figure 3 is a plot of the operating range versus signal loss in decibels (dB), with the point 1.0 on the x-axis of the graph representing the maximum range, whatever this may be in actual distance. It can be seen that a decrease of six dB in the received signal strength corresponds to an effective reduction of this range by one-half. A loss of 20 dB reduces the range by a factor of 10. This illustrates how drastically the operating range can vary from one situation to another, especially when it is realized that many things, such as building density, antenna types and orientations, and antenna position with respect to the body of the wearer, can all contribute losses of several dB. Thus, claims about operating range do not offer a reliable basis on which to compare equipment. The best procedure is to make comparative measurements under identical conditions. Only then can superior performance be recognized.

Batteries

Most body-worn transmitters and receivers can be equipped with a number of different types of batteries. Even though there are wide differences in their chemical composition, these batteries are near enough to the same physical shape and size that they may be interchanged or adapted to fit. This permits the user to select the best type for a particular application. Manufacturers of the equipment usually recommend the most advisable type to use. The importance of battery quality is paramount, and the user should insure that the use of poor batteries is avoided. Even recently purchased batteries may have already suffered sufficient shelf-life deterioration to cause significant degradation in the performance of a transmitter or receiver.

43

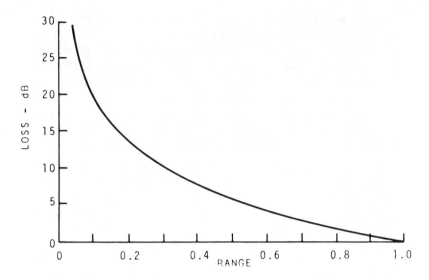

Figure 3. Normalized range as a function of signal loss in decibels.

With undercover surveillance equipment, such as body-worn transmitters and receivers, the most frequently used types of batteries are the alkaline and the mercury primary batteries. Nickel-cadmium, which are rechargeable, have not as yet found wide acceptance in undercover work. The carbon-zinc or common flashlight battery is generally not suitable because of its low capability of meeting high-current drain requirements. Alkaline and mercury batteries are desireable mainly because they are able to supply relatively large amounts of energy for their size. Alkaline batteries are less expensive and more readily available than mercury batteries. However, body transmitters using mercury batteries usually have a less rapid decay in power output (see Figures 11 and 17).

A good measure of the condition of a battery is its ability to sustain a moderate current drain. One test that may be used on a *9-volt alkaline* battery is to determine whether it will supply 75-80 milliamperes of current for a period of 45 seconds. This can be easily done using the circuit shown in Figure 4. If the battery is at an acceptable stage of charge, the voltmeter indication should not drop below 9 volts for a period of 45 seconds.

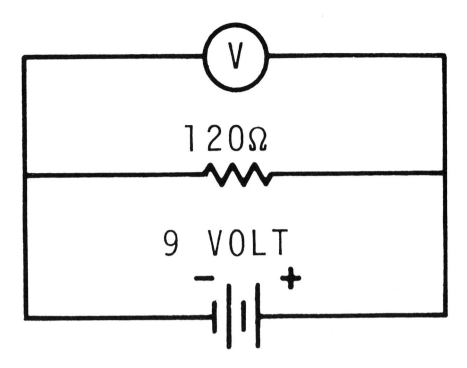

Figure 4. Battery test circuit.

It is not appropriate to test mercury batteries in the same manner because mercury batteries sustain a nearly constant voltage under load until they are almost completely discharged. Therefore, even though a mercury battery has undergone considerable use and is near the end of its lifetime, the current drain test might not indicate it. At present there appears to be no simple and reliable method for determining the state-of-charge of a mercury battery. Mercury batteries, fortunately, have a shelf life of approximately 2½ years. The best way to be confident of the freshness of a mercury battery is to make sure that its open terminal voltage is what it should be and to use batteries with fairly recent dates of manufacture. To avoid the possibility of battery failure during an operation requires vigilance. Points to remember about batteries include the following:

(a) Know the milliampere hours the battery can supply and the transmitter current drain.

(b) Make sure the batteries are fresh. If possible, use a fresh battery for each mission.

(c) Keep a log of battery life expended.

(d) For improved shelf-life, batteries should be stored at temperatures well below normal room temperature.

Neither the alkaline nor the mercury batteries are rechargeable and, once discharged, must be discarded. Care must be taken with mercury batteries to assure that they are not burned because toxic vapors are emitted which can endanger life. One further point regarding batteries is that their contents are corrosive and they should not be stored in an instrument for longer periods of time than necessary. Corrosion can cause serious damage to an expensive item of equipment.

Another important consideration is the effect of ambient temperature on battery operation and life. Some types of batteries suffer severe reductions in performance when subjected to either extreme heat or extreme cold. One example is the carbon-zinc (flashlight) battery, which suffers in its ability to perform when temperatures are below 0°C (32°F) or above 50°C (122°F). Also, the mercury battery is a poor performer at temperatures below 5°C (41°F), but is an excellent performer at high temperatures.

Crystal Control vs. Free-Running Oscillators

Undercover transmitters and receivers should be crystal-controlled because free running oscillators drift in frequency and can be changed by modulation, making it difficult to sustain optimum performance over long periods of time without retuning. Crystal-controlled equipment should operate with a frequency tolerance of a few parts per million. This tolerance varies with frequency; however, tolerances of 10 parts per million are typical in the 150 MHz range.

In some instances, the requirement for miniaturization may be so critical that the extra size incurred by the addition of crystal-controlled circuitry cannot be tolerated. In these situations, extremely small and very low-powered transmitters of a size comparable to a one-inch section of a common lead pencil can be used. In equipment this small, hearing aid batteries are used, and transmitter output is typically in the vicinity of 10 mW. Frequency drift in devices no having crystal control will typically be of the order of 10 kHz per hour under normal operating conditions.

Automatic Volume Control

It is evident that voice modulations reaching the transmitter will be at different intensities, depending on the proximity of the speaker to the microphone. The wearer of the transmitter will of course be much closer than the other speakers. Consequently, it is probable that the wearer's voice will be too loud while others may barely be heard. This brings about the critical need for automatic volume control circuitry in the transmitter so that all those talking may be heard distinctly.

Modulation and Audiofrequency Response

Because of circuit simplicity, good fidelity and the relatively low power drain, frequency modulation is used almost exclusively in undercover transmitters, although there appears to be no reason why other types of modulation could not be used in order to provide better security.

Most of the frequency components of the human voice are in the range from 300 Hz to 3000 Hz. This is the audiofrequency response for which the equipment should be designed. Broader responses are not only unnecessary but may even be detrimental, because sounds could be transmitted which may interfere with the intelligibility of the conversation being monitered.

Frequency Deviation

Federal Communications Commisiion (FCC) regulations pertaining to public safety communications equipment authorize a maximum frequency deviation of plus or minus five kHz for FM systems. It is important that surveillance transmitters be designed to satisfy this requirement, not solely because of the FCC regulations, but because the transmitters must be compatible with the receiving equipment commonly used in law enforcement communications. Clarity of reproduction is another reason for using equipment with the proper frequency deviation and modulation bandwidth. Using bandwidths narrower than those specified may create difficulty in identifying the speakers, while the use of broader bandwidths does not improve voice reproduction and may introduce unwanted sounds. It is particularly important that surveillance recordings be clear and intelligible because of their possible use as court evidence. In general, plus or minus five kHz frequency deviation and three kHz audiofrequency response provide adequate voice reproduction. In surveillance work, problems can arise related to the loudness of the modulating voices and the action of the automatic volume control (AVC) circuits, which may, in some cases, produce recordings unsuitable as court evidence.

Packaging

Miniature transmitters have been packaged and concealed in almost every way imaginable, as dictated by special needs. Lamps, plugs, chairlegs and flower pots have all been used to conceal a transmitter. Some have achieved fame and attracted international attention, such as the one concealed in the shoe of a diplomat and the one in the seal above the embassy desk. These are all custom-made devices, which for the most part would be unavailable to a police department unless it had direct contact with a facility which could produce them. Some of these devices are available, but information regarding specific suppliers is not easily obtained.

Good quality transmitters and receivers can be packaged in small, ruggedized containers with dimensions on the order of 7.5 cm x 5 cm x 2 cm (3" x 2" x ¾"), and can be either body worn or concealed in some unlikely location. The particular situation dictates the necessary concealment precautions and in this the agent must use his own judgement. If he cannot wear heavy clothing or outer garments, concealment may be a severe problem.

Electronic packaging has to be considered, especially in the sense that the devices used should be repairable and the circuitry should be accessible for trouble shooting purposes. Devices which are potted in an epoxy envelope, although weatherproof, are not repairable in the event of circuit failure. It is characteristically the very low-priced and lower quality devices that are manufactured in this way. Epoxy-potted transmitters usually operate in the 100 to 120 MHz range.

Ease of Detection

Detection may occur by visual observation, physical search (frisking), or by the use of electronic defensive (countermeasures) equipment. Little can be said of the likelihood of detection by visual or physical means except that the smaller the device is, the less apt it is to be discovered. Obviously, discovery is dependent upon how cleverly it is concealed.

Detection by electronic methods deserves more thorough attention. Consider the following three factors for the bearing they have on detection:

Operating Frequency: As has already been mentioned, transmitters operating in the 88 to 108 MHz band are more apt to be detected due to the fact that receivers covering this band are extremely common. It does not require a very vivid imagination to picture an undercover agent in a situation where someone is tuning through this frequency band and picks up the broadcast of voices and sounds from within the room, or hears the oscillatory squeal of energy feedback to the receiver by a concealed transmitter. These frequencies should be avoided.

Power Output: High power output increases the operating range. But the greater the power radiated, the wider the area of coverage, with the consequence that detection is more probable. Therefore, it is advisable to avoid using a one-watt transmitter, for example, where a one-quarter-watt unit would do. Where there is a reasonable choice, it is much wiser to improve receiver sensitivity or antenna efficiency than to increase transmitter power.

Harmonics: Good equipment radiates energy primarily at the fundamental frequency, and filters out and supresses the harmonics. This makes it less likely that the energy being radiated will affect other equipment, such as television receivers, which may draw suspicion and lead to discovery. It is not unreasonable to expect the level of radiated harmonic and other spurious energy to be at least 35 dB below that of the fundamental output of the transmitter. Devices may be discovered by detection of the energy radiated at their harmonic frequencies because antenna efficiency may be better at the harmonic frequencies than it is at the fundamental frequency. Searching by electronic methods is often done by starting at the high-frequency region and working downward.

Antennas

Overall system performance can be greatly affected by the type of antenna used, the type of installation, and the conditions of operation. Monopole antennas are used exclusively with body-worn transmitters, because they are omnidirectional and of very simple construction. For many reasons, other antenna configurations are impractical.

One important fact to consider is that best communication usually occurs between two monopole antennas when they are oriented parallel to one another; i.e., polarization should be the same in both antennas. Either they both should be vertical or both horizontal. Although this is generally true, local distortions in field configuration caused by conducting objects such as steel in a building can cause significant variations.

Normally, the optimum length for an omnidirectional monopole antenna is approximately one-quarter wavelength at the operating frequency. However, this is modified somewhat in the case of antennas placed next to the body. Because of the added capacitance between the antenna and the body of the wearer, resonance occurs when the length of the antenna is four or five percent shorter than one wavelength.

The requirements that the antenna be both small and located next to the body constitute very severe handicaps to efficient communication. Antennas that are short compared to a quarter wavelength are not efficient. In addition, the human body is a good absorber of radio energy. These constraints combine to place very severe limitations on the distances over which satisfactory communication can be achieved. Given ideal antenna conditions, it is entirely possible to maintain good communication with transmitters of one-watt or less at distances of several miles. However, when antennas are shortened and placed next to the body, the range may drop to a few hundred feet or less, depending on local propagation conditions.

Propagation Conditions

The propagation medium is an important component of the communications system. This is the part of the system over which the operator has almost no control. An accurate prediction of how well a system will work when in a given situation is not possible to any high degree of acuracy without actually making field strength measurements. This is usually impractical, so the next best thing is to examine some of the variables and do those things which will enhance the probability of success.

Two factors which affect the performance of an antenna are the conductivity and the dielectric constant of the ground. These vary widely around the country, and can make a difference in field strength of as much as several dB. The moisture content of the soil is also a factor, as higher amounts of moisture enhance propagation. While these factors are not controllable, they are mentioned for general interest.

Some factors are controllable by the operators. One way to improve the received signal from a verticle monopole is to elevate the receiving antenna. Improvements of several decibels in received signal strength can be realized by choosing listening post locations so that the angle between transmitter and receiver is 30 to 45 degrees from the horizontal.

A transmitter or receiver does not perform well when placed inside an automobile. The metal enclosure acts as a shield which attenuates high-frequency electromagnetic energy. If there were no windows in the car, or an outside antenna, there would be essentially no transmission at all. The metal used as building reinforcement also reduces the strength of a transmitted signal. Even the average home may seriously hamper inside-to-outside communication because of the use of foil-backed insulation in the walls. A transmitter enclosed in a metal container is completely ineffective. This fact was once used in an extortion case involving a money drop. The criminal, suspecting that a transmitter was concealed in the package, placed it in a metal suitcase and thereby escaped because the transmitter was useless. The wearer of a transmitter may position himself near openings such as non-metallic doors or windows, thereby avoiding the shielding effects of unseen metal barriers. The use of such tactics comes with experience and a general understanding of the behavior of radio energy.

Body-Mounted Transmitters

There are a number of other features which may be important in the field use of body-mounted transmitters and these are discussed below.

Polarity Protection

When installing batteries in a body-mounted transmitter, it is very important that the batteries be oriented for correct polarity. Most units employ alkaline batteries equipped with snap-on connectors. These batteries cannot be installed with the incorrect polarity because the connectors at the positive and negative terminals are different from each other and the battery will not fit the receptacle unless it is correctly oriented.

Occasionally a body-worn transmitter may be encountered which utilizes mercury batteries. A group of four or five individual cells are usually held in place by a cardboard or plastic sleeve, and two such groups are required to power the transmitter. Because mercury cells are not equipped with snap-on connectors like the alkaline batteries, it is possible to install them with reversed polarity.

There are at least two possible consequences of imposing the incorrect voltage polarity. First, the transmitter will not operate and the operator may not know why. Next, the transmitter may be permanently damaged. This can happen with either the mercury or alkaline batteries because even a very brief, momentary exposure to reversed polarity can result in irreversible damage. Whether or not such damage will result depends on the circuit, and better quality units have built in polarity protection.

Antenna Connector

A common trouble spot in body-worn transmitters is the connector between the antenna lead and the transmitter. A wide variety of connectors are used by various manufacturers and most have both advantages and disadvantages. There are the simple plug-in microphone jack types, the screw-on types, and the twist-lock types. Two considerations are important. First is the possibility that the lead will be pulled out of the socket during use, will work loose, or will otherwise break the connection. Second is the ease of making repairs if the antenna lead is broken. Some units combine the microphone wire and the antenna wire into one lead.

Microphone

Although microphones will be discussed in detail in a later section, it is worthy to note here that two different mounting schemes are used. Some miniature transmitters have the microphone built into the case of the transmitter, while others use a microphone connected by a cable. If the microphone is mounted in the case, there should be a dirt seal to protect it against clogging and subsequent damage or loss of sensitivity. A piece of foam-like material is a satisfactory protector for this purpose.

Most of the better transmitters use the electrodynamic type of microphone, which has excellent sensitivity and adequate frequency response for voice communication. Electret microphones of adequate quality are a relatively recent development. They provide better frequency response and may be expected to find increased use in undercover equipment. Both types are rugged, but electret microphones have a limited lifetime of about three years of operation at maximum sensitivity. Should this be overcome and costs made competitive with the electrodynamic types, electret microphones could come into common use.

Location of On-Off Switch

Because miniature transmitters are often located where they are subject to being jolted, or where other materials may rub against them, it is important that the on-off switch be of a positive type requiring a fairly strong force to operate and that it be in a location where it is not apt to be moved accidentally. In some situations it may be desireable to make it either difficult or impossible for the wearer to turn the switch off while the surveillance operation is under way. Some manufacturers make special provisions for this but may not indicate it in their specifications.

Ruggedness

Body-worn equipment should be constructed to withstand severe physical shocks. Construction should be such that dropping from chest height to a concrete floor will not permanently affect operation. This requires either an all-metal case of heavy guage or a very high performance plastic. If plastic materials are used, they should not soften when warm or shatter in severe cold.

Size

The primary factor limiting the smallness of a transmitter is the size of the batteries required to supply the power. In general, a crystal-controlled transmitter with batteries, having an output in the 0.2 to 1 watt range, can be contained in a volume slightly smaller than a cigarette package. In such a transmitter, the batteries occupy approximately 75 percent of total volume, and the crystal-control feature adds additional bulk. Transmitters no larger than the eraser portion of a common lead pencil are available, but these devices are not crystal-controlled, have a power output of only a milliwatt or so, and their greater frequency instability restricts their application and dependability. Such low-power transmitters are not suitable for applications where they must be placed next to a large power absorber such as the human body. They may be used as room bugs where long distances to listening posts are not involved.

Receivers

Receivers used in undercover work are not always packaged in miniaturized form because in many instances concealment is not required. The sensitivity of a receiver has almost nothing to do with its physical size. Receiver components and measurable characteristics which distinguish good quality equipment from poor quality equipment are discussed below.

Sensitivity

Sensitivity is probably the most important characteristic of receiver quality. It is a measure of how weak a signal can be detected, and therefore is of first-order importance in determining the operating range of an undercover receiver. There are two common methods of specifying this information. The first is in terms of microvolts for 20 dB quieting. The second is in terms of microvolts for 12 dB SINAD. Either is an acceptable method, although the 12 dB SINAD provides a better measure of true receiver performance because it is made under modulated conditions. As a general rule of thumb, one may add 0.1 microvolt to the 12 dB SINAD sensitivity figure to obtain a comparable sensitivity for a receiver rated on the basis of 20 dB quieting. Although this is not exact, it does provide a quick means of comparing two receivers which are specified in these different ways. For example, a good receiver should be capable of at least 0.4 microvolt sensitivity at 12 dB SINAD or 0.5 microvolts for 20 dB quieting.

Frequency Control

The receiver should be equipped with a crystal-controlled local oscillator for automatic frequency control. Otherwise it will tend to drift or detune, causing fading of the received signal. This is especially important if the receiver is to be unattended for extended periods of time.

Adjacent Channel Rejection

Adjacent channel rejection, also termed selectivity, is achieved through the use of good filter networks which reject signals at nearby frequencies, preventing unwanted interference.

Antenna

Much the same considerations apply to receiving antennas as to transmitting antennas, particularly if they are worn on the body. Where the receiver is not body-worn, one would normally use antennas which have higher gains and/or directives.

Advantages and Disadvantages of Body-Worn Transmitters and Receivers

Advantages:

1. Completely portable (small and lightweight).
2. Quickly installed.
3. Highly versatile.

Disadvantages:

1. Limited period of operation.
2. Limited and uncertain range of operation.
3. Can be located by electromagnetic sensors.

4. Will not relay information when surrounded by a conducting shield such as a car body, airplane, or metal suitcase.
5. Quality (intelligibility) of transmitted information may vary.
6. Subject to locally generated interference and atmospheric noise.
7. Personal contact with subject often necessary.

TESTS OF RADIATING DEVICES

Laboratory Tests of Body-Worn Transmitters

A limited number of measurements were performed to evaluate some of the equipment which is now commercially available to law enforcement agencies for electronic surveillance work. Five transmitters were tested to determine some of their operating characteristics. All units were of the FM crystal-controlled type, operating on either mercury or alkaline batteries and capable of output powers of 1 watt or less.

The units were tested for frequency stability, output power as a function of time, spurious emissions, AM hum and noise, and dc current drain and efficiency.

The testing was performed under laboratory conditions of approximately 23° C (73°F) and 40 percent relative humidity, with each transmitter radiating into a 50 ohm load. Table 1 shows some of the test results. Others are described below. The following units were tested:

#1 Nominal rf output 1 watt, carrier frequency 165.188 MHz, frequency modulated, powered by three 4.2 volt mercury batteries.

#2 Nominal rf output 250 milliwatts, carrier frequency 165.188 MHz, frequency modulated, powered by three 4.2 volt mercury batteries.

#3 Nominal rf output 250 milliwatts, carrier frequency 151.625 MHz, frequency modulated, powered by two 7-volt mercury batteries.

#4 Nominal rf output 10 milliwatts, carrier frequency 159.300 MHz, frequency modulated, powered by one 9-volt alkaline battery.

#5 Nominal rf output 25 milliwatts, carrier frequency 154.890 MHz, phase modulated, powered by one 9-volt alkaline battery.

#6 Nominal rf output 100 milliwatts, carrier frequency 154.890 MHz, frequency modulated, powered by one 9-volt alkaline battery.

Units #1, #2 and #3 were designed for body-worn use, while units #4 and #5 were designed for stationary application in a building to provide security against holdups. Therefore, a direct comparison of the first three units with units #4 and #5 is not appropriate. All units were comparable in size to a cigarette package and therefore could be concealed on a person. With regard to Table 1, the harmonic suppression is the difference in signal strength between the fundamental output frequency of the transmitter and the next most powerful component of the radiated spectrum. It is desireable that this difference be as large as possible; thus, the larger numbers indicate better performance. Spectrum-pictures of the ouput of the five transmitters are shown in Figures 6, 8, 10, 12 and 14. AM hum and noise is a measure of the undesired amplitude modulation produced within the transmitter, and again the larger numbers indicate better performance. The efficiency values given in the last row were calculated from the relationship,

$$E = \frac{P_{rf}}{P_{dc}} \times 100$$

where P_{rf} is the rf power of the transmitter and P_{dc} is the product of the dc current and dc voltage supplied by the transmitter batteries. The dc voltage and rf power data are shown graphically in Figures 5, 7, 9, 11 and 15.

Transmitter #1

Figure 5 shows the decay in rf output power due to the expenditure of battery energy over the operating period.

Parameter	Transmitter				
	#1	#2	#3	#4	#5
Frequency stability parts per million.	3 ppm over period of 4 hr. 45 min.	5 ppm over period of 2 hr. 45 min.	5 ppm over period of 3 hr. 45 min.	6 ppm over period of 3 hr. 45 min.	1 ppm over period of 45 min.
Harmonic suppression.	33 dB	33 dB	31 dB	6 dB	30 dB
AM hum and noise..	57.7 dB	52.8 dB	50.1 dB	24.9 dB	25.1 dB
D.C. current............	230 ma at 10.0 volts	97.8 ma at 9.3 volts	56 ma at .11.0 volts	34 ma at 9.3 volts	74 ma at 9.3 volts
Efficiency into 50 Ω load	65.9%	32.4%	34.1%	2.6%	6.2%

Table 1. Laboratory Test Results

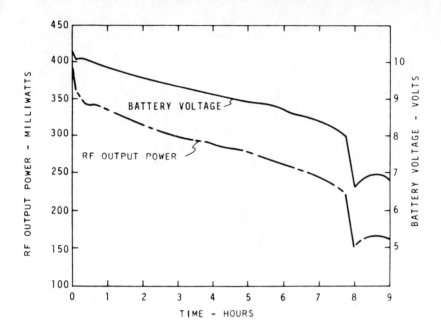

Figure 7. Decay of output power and battery voltage for transmitter #2.

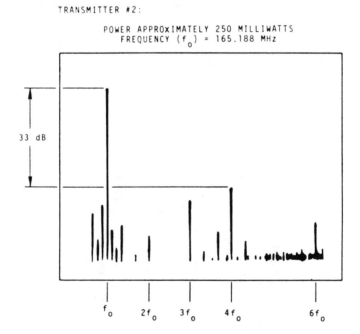

TRANSMITTER #2:

POWER APPROXIMATELY 250 MILLIWATTS
FREQUENCY (f_0) = 165.188 MHz

33 dB

f_0 $2f_0$ $3f_0$ $4f_0$ $6f_0$

Figure 8. Output spectrum of transmitter #2.

60

Also shown on the same graph is the battery voltage variation over the same time period. The output power was nearly constant for the first half hour and did not fall below the half-power point until approximately 2½ hours of operation. Three 4.2 volt mercury batteries were used to power the transmitter, and it appears that a cell failure may have occurred in one of the batteries near the end of the first hour. This would explain the rather significant drop in output power over the next thirty minutes of operation. This performance is apparently not typical, as is indicated by the data from the other transmitters. However, it does illustrate what can happen and shows how critical battery performance is to reliable operation. The output spectrum of this transmitter, shown in Figure 6, remained essentially the same over a 3-hour period.

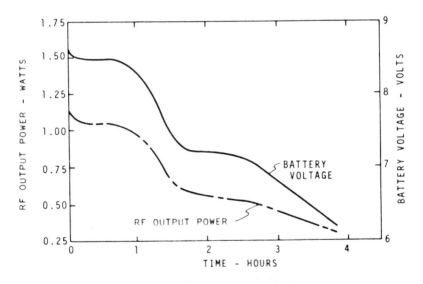

Figure 5. Decay of output power and battery voltage for transmitter #1.

Transmitter #2

As shown in Figure 7, the decay in transmitter output was approximately linear after the first few minutes of operation, and the half-power output level was not reached until after 8 hours of operation. A cell failure appears to have occurred at approximately 7 hours and 45 minutes into the test. The batteries were three 4.2 volt mercury batteries of the same type and manufacturer as those used in the test of transmitter #1. This would appear to be typical of the expected performance. Figure 8 shows the output spectrum with the strongest spurious radiation being the fourth harmonic (660 MHz), which is approximately 33 dB lower than the fundamental carrier frequency output, f_o.

TRANSMITTER #1:

POWER APPROXIMATELY 1 WATT
FREQUENCY (f_o) = 165.188 MHz

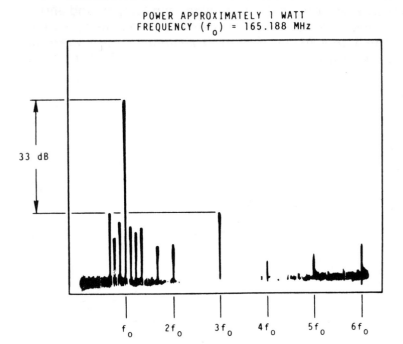

Figure 6. Output spectrum of transmitter #1.

Transmitter #3

Referring to Figure 9, it is apparent that the behavior of transmitter #3 was much the same as that of transmitter #2. Operation time to half-power output level was nearly the same, and a cell failure occurred after approximately

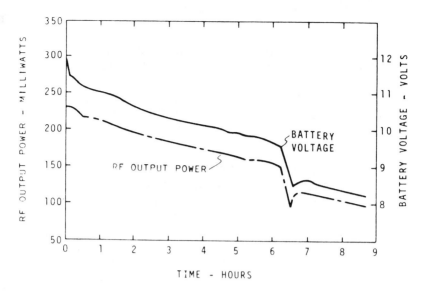

Figure 9. Decay of output power and battery voltage for transmitter #3.

TRANSMITTER #3:

POWER APPROXIMATELY 250 MILLIWATTS
FREQUENCY (f_0) = 151.625 MHz

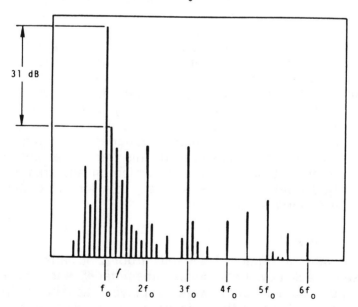

Figure 10. Output spectrum of transmitter #3.

63

6 hours and 15 minutes. The output spectrum (Fig. 10) shows the spurious radiation to be down approximately 31 dB below the fundamental. In contrast to transmitters #1 and #2, the most intense spurious radiation was evidently not a harmonic of the fundamental frequency.

Transmitter #4

One 9-volt carbon-zinc battery served as the dc supply for this transmitter, and its performance was noticeably different from those of transmitters #1, 2 and 3, which used mercury batteries. Transmitter #4 was received in a poorly adjusted condition, as can be seen from Figures 11 and 12. For this reason the spurious radiation level was only 6 dB below the fundamental carrier frequency output (Fig. 12). In this condition, this transmitter would be unacceptable for undercover work because of the ease with which it could be detected by its excessive spurious radiation. Elimination of unwanted spurious radiation wastes power; when a bandpass filter was inserted between the transmitter and the power meter to eliminate the spurious energy, the output showed a very significant drop. This is shown by the curves labeled case 1 and case 2 in figure 11. Compared to other transmitters using mercury batteries, it is apparent that a rather large initial drop in output power occurs soon after the turn-on when using carbon-zinc batteries, although the decay rate after the first hour or so appears to be comparable. also, the mercury batteries do not appear to suffer the radical voltage drops under load evidenced by the carbon-zinc batteries. It should be noticed that the efficiencies of this transmitter and of transmitter #5 are quite low, which means that the radiated output energies are very low for the battery powers being expended.

Transmitter #5

As with transmitter #4, a 9-volt carbon-zinc battery was used as a dc power source for transmitter #5, and similar output characteristics were displayed, as shown in Figure 13. However, the initial decay in output power was

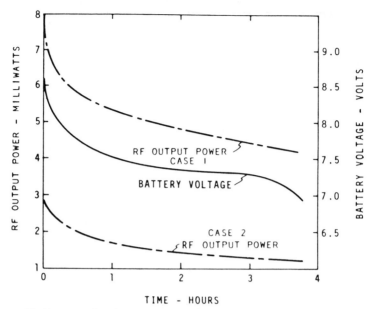

Figure 11. Decay of output power and battery voltage for transmitter #4.

TRANSMITTER #4:

POWER APPROXIMATELY 7 MILLIWATTS
FREQUENCY (f_0) = 159.300 MHz

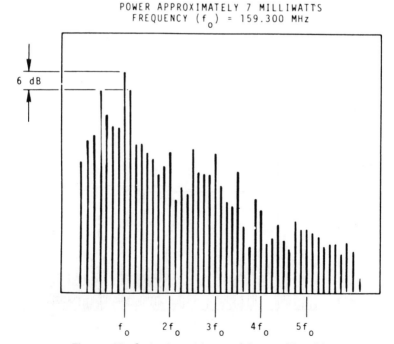

Figure 12. Output spectrum of transmitter #4.

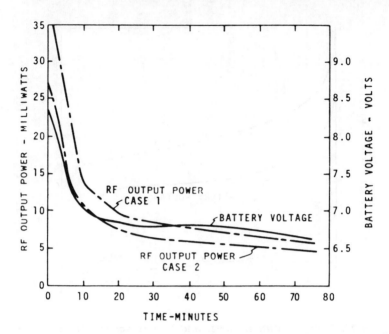

Figure 13. Decay of output power and battery voltage for transmitter #5.

TRANSMITTER #5:

POWER APPROXIMATELY 25 MILLIWATTS
FREQUENCY (f_o) = 154.890 MHz

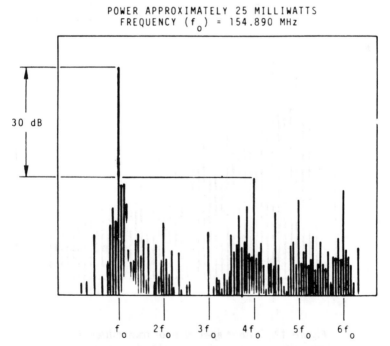

Figure 14. Output spectrum of transmitter #5.

so severe that a half power level was reached after only a few minutes of operation. Such a transmitter might serve satisfactorily for short and intermittent use but would be unsatisfactory for most undercover missions. As with transmitter #4, a bandpass filter was inserted and the change in output power noted. Because the spurious radiation was an acceptable 30 dB below the carrier output (see Fig. 14), there was a much less severe change in the output upon insertion of the filter, as is illustrated by the similarity between the curves of case 1 and case 2.

Carbon-zinc batteries are not recomended to power transmitters in undercover surveillance use because of their inability to provide adequate power. Both mercury and alkaline batteries are much more satisfactory.

Transmitter #6

The sixth transmitter was tested to assess the difference in transmitter performance as a function of the type of battery used. It was operated until it reached its half-power output levels, first with a carbon-zinc battery and then with an alkaline battery. Figure 15 is a plot of the resulting data and shows a half-power lifetime of slightly more than 1½ hours using the alkaline battery compared to only 15 minutes with the carbon-zinc battery. The performance of mercury batteries is similar to that of the alkaline.

Field Tests of Body-Worn Transmitters

When the antenna of a transmitter is mounted on a human body, the effective radiated power of the transmitter is considerably reduced. To study this phenomenon, an outdoor test range was established and measurements were made under simulated field conditions. The data thus gathered are very interesting, and illustrate the amount of variation and the complexity of the problem of maintaining dependable communication using body-worn equipment.

The measurement set-up, using a field strength meter at the receiver location, is illustrated in Figure 16.

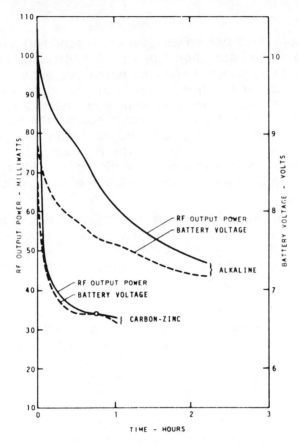

Figure 15. Decay of output power of transmitter #6 using alkaline and carbon-zinc batteries.

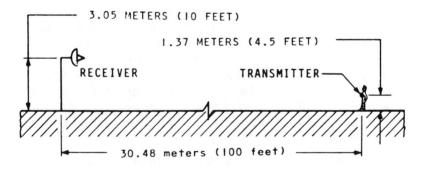

Figure 16.
Test setup for field performance studies of body-worn transmitters.

Transmitter #1, described above, was used. Measurements were made in the daytime under warm, dry conditions, and there were no buildings or other obstructions in the area. Initial measurements were made with the transmitter and its antenna mounted on a wooden post, with the transmitter and receiver antennas oriented vertically. A series of measurements were then made with the transmitter and its antenna mounted in various locations on a person with the person oriented at different angles to the receiving antenna. In all cases, the first position was with the subject facing the receiver with arms extended downward at the sides. Succeeding observations were made with the subject rotated clockwise to the successive 90 degree positions. To observe the changes in field strength due to arm movement, the arms were moved through a variety of positions including extending them directly overhead, to the front, and to the sides. The arm movements followed a consistent pattern of continuous motion during which the field strength fluctuations were observed on the meter. These fluctuations are shown for measurements two through six; the approximate variation of the field strength reading is indicated for each of the four facing positions. In some instances, arm movement appeared to increase signal strength perceptibly. The measurement conditions and data observed were as follows (observed field strengths at the receiver are given in dB above one microvolt per meter):

Measurement #1: Transmitter mounted on a vertical wooden post with transmitting and receiving antennas vertical. The observed field strength was 91.4 dB uV/m.

Measurement #2: The transmitter was mounted on the under belt at approximately waist level (see Fig. 17). The antenna extended up the left side of the chest to the shoulder. The subject was wearing a cotton "T-shirt." The subject was then oriented at the four quadrant angles to the transmitter, and the variations due to arm movements were noted at each position. The transmitting and receiving antennas were oriented vertically.

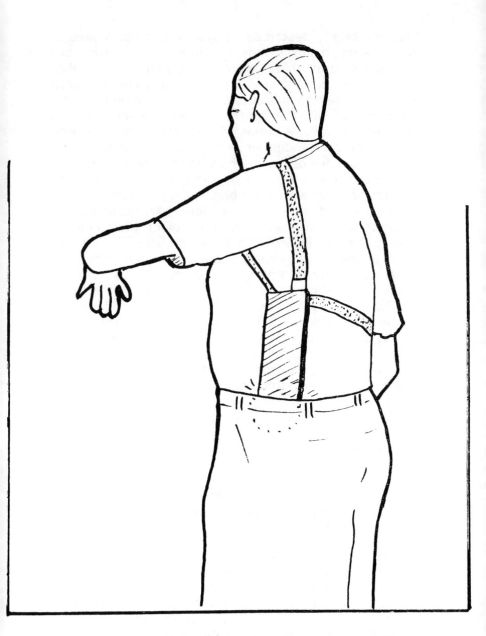

Figure 17. Transmitter position for measurement #2.

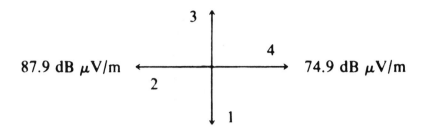

88.9 dB μV/m

87.9 dB μV/m   74.9 dB μV/m

71.4 dB μV/m

Facing receiver — arms down in all positions

Changes in field strength, E, with arm movement

Position	Variation (dB)
1	−12 to +8
2	− 4 to +1
3	− 4 to +1
4	− 4 to +1

Measurement #3: The transmitter was tucked into the belt with the antenna positioned vertically up the center of the chest over a "T-shirt" (see Fig. 18).

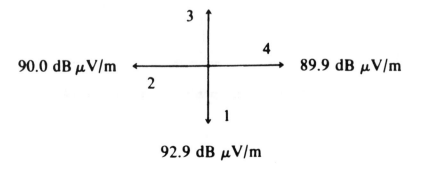

69.9 dB μV/m

90.0 dB μV/m   89.9 dB μV/m

92.9 dB μV/m

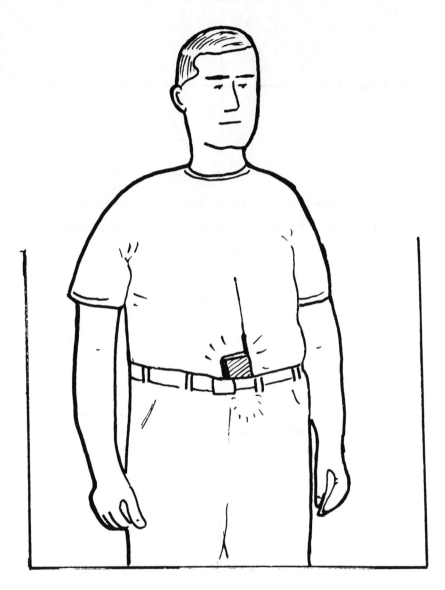

Figure 18. Transmitter position for measurement #3.

Facing receiver — arms down in all positions

Changes in field strength, E, with arm movement

Position	Variation (dB)
1	−6 to 0
2	−7 to +1
3	0 to +10
4	−7 to +1

Measurement #4: The transmitter was tucked into the belt with the antenna arranged vertically up the center of the chest next to the skin.

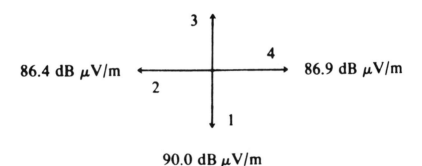

67.9 dB μV/m

86.4 dB μV/m   86.9 dB μV/m

90.0 dB μV/m

Facing receiver — arms down in all positions

Changes in field strength, E, with arm movement

Position	Variation (dB)
1	−3 to +1
2	−10 to +2
3	−6 to +6
4	−10 to +2

Measurement #5: Both the transmitter and receiver antennas were oriented horizontally. The transmitter location was at the waist, with the antenna wrapped around the waist just above the belt.

76.4 dB μV/m

```
                    3  ↑
                                4
84.9 dB μV/m   ←────────┼────────→   81.9 dB μV/m
                2       │
                        │
                        ↓  1
```

89.9 dB μV/m

Facing receiver — arms down in all positions

Changes in field strength, E, with arm movement

Position	Variation (dB)
1	−0.5 to 0
2	0 to +5
3	−8 to +2
4	−7 to +1

Measurement #6: The transmitter antenna was oriented horizontally and the receiver antenna was oriented vertically. The transmitter and its antenna were mounted at the waist in the same manner as for measurement #5.

74

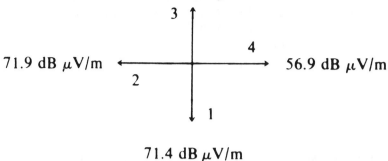

51.9 dB μV/m

71.9 dB μV/m   3   4   56.9 dB μV/m

2

1

71.4 dB μV/m

Facing receiver — arms down in all positions

Changes in field strength, E, with arm movement

Position	Variation (dB)
1	−9 to +1
2	−9 ro +1
3	0 to +13
4	0 to +13

Measurement #7: Both the transmitter and receiver antennas were oriented vertically, with the transmitter mounted on the left hip of the subject and the antenna extended down the thigh toward the knee.

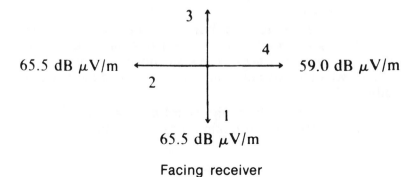

64.0 dB μV/m

65.5 dB μV/m   3   4   59.0 dB μV/m

2

1

65.5 dB μV/m

Facing receiver

Measurement #8: The conditions were identical to those in #7 except that the transmitter was mounted at the knee of the subject and the antenna extended down the lower leg toward the ankle.

71.0 dB μV/m

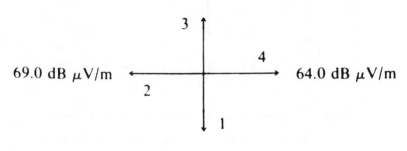

69.0 dB μV/m

Note that measurements #1 through #6 were made on one day and measurements #7 and #8 were made on a second day. This allows the possibility that the radiated power from the transmitter might not have been equal on the two days. Therefore, it is not certain that upper-body mounting of the transmitter provides a larger signal, as the data would seem to indicate.

Although these data are by no means conclusive, several tentative conclusions can be drawn:

(1) When the body is between the transmitting and receiving antennas, there is a very significant reduction in the strength of the received signal. Therefore, the wearer should make every effort to keep himself oriented so that his transmitting antenna is on the same side of his body as the receiver.

(2) It is desireable to have the receiving antenna oriented parallel to the transmitting antenna. The data of measurement #6 show severe signal loss (approximately 25 dB) when the two antennas are perpendicular to each other.

(3) Arm movement is significant and can have a very important effect when communication is marginal. It is

best to keep the arms as far away from the antenna as possible. Folding the arms across the chest-mounted antenna could attenuate a signal enough to make it unrecoverable.

NONRADIATING DEVICES

General

The distinguishing feature of nonradiating surveillance devices is the medium used to convey information from one location to another. The information is transmitted over wires, usually telephone wires, instead of being broadcast.

Wired surveillance systems have several distinct advantages over radiating systems. Most notable is the security from detection by an electronic sweep made by a radio receiver. Because virtually no electromagnetic energy is radiated from the wired network, this means of discovery is eliminated. A second very important consideration is the virtually unlimited range that is possible. Although the range of radiating devices is usually measured in feet, the range of wired systems can be measured in miles. In addition, wired communication systems include a source of dc voltage. Many wired surveillance devices use this built-in voltage source to eliminate the troublesome and limiting battery requirement. A final advantage which can not be overlooked is the reliability of the communication medium. Wires are not affected by atmospheric conditions, and signals of consistent and dependable quality are almost always certain, with the additional benefit that natural and man-made radiation interference are eliminated.

While wired systems have many advantages, they also have limitations. Restricted mobility is most often the reason a wired surveillance system is not used. In cases where the person under surveillance is on the move or located away from a fixed listening post, the use of wired equipment is obviously not feasible. A second drawback is that prior access to the premises is required to install listening devices or telephone taps. Also, in most instances, more advanced preparation time is needed to set up wired equipment, so it is difficult to respond quickly to emergencies. Where these restrictions pose insurmountable problems, there is no choice but to use radiating devices.

In some states there are laws which prohibit telephone tapping. Therefore, portable and body-worn transmitters and receivers are essentially the only undercover communications devices available to law enforcement officers for electronic surveillance.

Concealed Microphones

Microphones cannot be found by electromagnetic searching devices. The only means of discovery is through physical search. Installation requires access to the premises, but the degree of concealment is limited only by the immagination of the installer, the cleverness of his methods, and the time he has to work. The basic equipment required consists of a microphone as small as possible, the necessary length of shielded wire, and a tape recorder. Shielded wire is used where possible to avoid unwanted pickup, such as power line hum or other noise coupled into the circuit. For short lead lengths, very fine wires can be run along baseboards, window sills, or under floor coverings. Conducting paint can be used to form a conducting path on a wall surface. This is done by simply painting thin conducting stripes on the surface as required, and making electrical connections at the ends of the painted stripes. These stripes can then be painted over with regular paint, making discovery difficult.

Excellent microphones as small as 10 mm x 7 mm x 5 mm (⅜" x ¼" x ³/₁₆") are available, with sensitivities such that they can pick up a whisper at approximately 7.5 meters (25 feet). These can be combined with an amplifier of comparable size so that a listening post can be established several miles away, using a pair of unused telephone wires.

The small dynamic-type microphones commonly used for these purposes require a column of air (a leak) directly in front of the pick-up surface so that, in mounting them, a very small hole must be drilled in the object used for concealment. Sometimes, plastic tubing threaded through a crack serves this purpose and aids in concealment. Microphones equipped with a small section of metal tube directly over the microphone leak are available for attaching the tubing.

In the use of a microphone for eavesdropping, it is important that precautions be taken to avoid rubbing against the microphone because this introduces noise. This becomes a problem especially when a microphone is used with a body-worn transmitter which is hidden in clothing. Friction from cloth rubbing against the microphone is called "clothes noise" and poses a problem in obtaining good quality sound reproduction.

Miniature surveillance microphones, with their amplifiers, have characteristics similar to those of the human ear. The fact that the ear and the microphone can detect the same sound at the same distance provides a guide to the limits of a physical search for a hidden microphone. There are devices such as the highly directional shotgun or parabolic microphones which have greater ranges, but they are much more difficult to conceal. These instruments can detect normal conversation at ranges of 50 to 100 feet. Their increased range is derived from their directionality and, for some, their acoustic amplification. This directionality prevents interference from any direction other than that in which the device is pointed. One defense against such devices is to add background sounds, such as music. This, along with speaking in low voices, can render the recorded conversation unintelligible.

Microphone technology is an extensive field, and no attempt will be made to cover the subject in depth. However, several types of microphones which are of special interest in electronic surveillance, and which find fairly wide application, will be described briefly.

Carbon Microphones

The carbon microphone is the type used in the mouthpiece of a telephone transmitter. It operates on the principle that the resistance of a package of carbon granules varies as the external pressure on the package changes. When mounted behind a vibrating diaphragm and energized with a dc voltage, the carbon microphone will cause the current in the circuit to vary in accordance with the sound striking the diaphragm. The modulating effect enables the voice to be transmitted over the telephone circuit. Carbon microphones are very sensitive but have a rather high background noise of the hiss type. They do not lend themselves to miniaturization as well as other types of microphones.

Condenser Microphone

Also referred to as an electrostatic microphone, the condenser microphone uses a vibrating diaphragm as one plate of a parallel-plate, air-dialectic capacitor. Sound striking the diaphragm produces capacitance variations which, in turn, produce electrical impulses. Condenser microphones can be made very senstive and reproduce sound with excellent fidelity, but they have the disadvantages of being fragile and sensitive to vibrations transmitted through solids. For these reasons, they are generally not suitable for eavesdropping applications.

Electrodynamic Microphones

Often called simply a dynamic microphone, this is the type most commonly used in electronic surveillance. These microphones have many desireable features. They can be very small, adequately sensitive, rugged, and require no external power source. The modulated current is generated by means of a coil of wire in the field of a permanent magnet.

Electret Microphone

Recent technology has resulted in the development of miniature electret microphones which have many features useful in electronic surveillance work. An electret is the electrical analog to a permanent magnet. A permanently polarized dielectric material which is sensitive to pressure changes produced by acoustic energy is used as the sensing element. Operation is similar to that of the condenser microphone, but the electret microphone is much more resistant to shock and solid-borne vibration. Advantages of the electret are that no external bias is required, and it has a frequency response which is superior to those of other types. Superior frequency response, however, is not of first-order importance in electronic surveillance, where only voice frequencies are of interest. Electrets perform well under temperature extremes and may be slightly superior from the standpoint of ruggedness, but one precautionary note is worthy of mention. While it appears that better materials are being developed which will diminish the problem, periods of humidity in the range of 90 percent or more cause drastic loss of sensitivity. Should this problem be overcome and costs made competitive with those of the dynamic types, the electret may become the preferred type of microphone. At present, however, the electret appears to be little used, and it may be several years before this situation changes.

Induction Microphone

The induction microphone is very similar in principle of operation to the electrodynamic microphone in that both incorporate a moving conductor in the field of a permanent magnet. The induction microphone uses a fixed coil and a moving piece of magnetic material, whereas the electromagnetic type employs a moving coil and is often much smaller. A common example of the induction microphone is the ear piece of a telephone. These microphones are sometimes used as room bugs where concealment problems do not require a device as small as the electrodynamic type. Because they are used in telephones, they are inexpensive and readily available; this explains their common use.

Advantages

1. Unlimited range.
2. Operating time not limited by battery life.
3. Not subject to radiated electromagnetic interference.
4. Not detectable by electromagnetic sensors.
5. Personal contact with subject not required.

Disadvantages

1. Prior access to premises required.
2. Lack of mobility.
3. Outlawed in some states, court order required in others to use telephone system.
4. Installation requires highly skilled people.

TAPE RECORDERS

In gathering legal evidence through electronic surveillance, the tape recorder is an indispensible item. Whether the surveillance method is a radiating system involving transmitters and receivers or a wired system using a telephone tap or a concealed microphone, a tape recorder is invariably involved. Many very good tape recorders are available, but there are apparently none designed specifically for surveillance purposes. In general, most good tape recorders are adequate to perform the functions required by electronic surveillance, especially in regard to sensitivity and frequency response. Both open-reel and cassette-type recorders are used.

Open-Reel Tape Recorders

The main advantage of the open-reel recorder is its large tape capacity, which allows for very long periods of recording without the necessity of changing reels. It generally yields broader frequency response, but this is not required for good fidelity in voice reproduction since the voice frequency band is relatively narrow. Important options available on open-reel recorders include voice-actuation, and automatic shut-off at the end of a reel so that tape flap noise will not reveal the presence of a hidden recorder. Temperature extremes are to be avoided; the temperature inside the trunk of an automobile on a hot day, for example, can cause serious operational difficulties.

Cassete Tape Recorders

The cassette is being used increasingly in spite of its smaller recording capacity. This is due to the advantages of small size and ease of operation; it is much quicker and easier to change and handle the tape. Miniature versions of the cassette tape recorder are now making their appearance, and at least one model is available which is small enough for concealment within clothing, its dimensions being 5 cm x 7.5 cm x 2.5 cm (2" x 3" x 1"). This will have a significant bearing on the application of recorders and could conceivably displace radiating equipment in certain situations.

CONCLUSIONS AND RECOMMENDATIONS

There are several standards available to guage the quality and performance of personal/portable electronic equipment. However, there is a degree of uniqueness about electronic surveillance equipment which would seem to require standards especially tailored for these devices. As an example, since battery life is so citrically important in the case of body-worn transmitters, it follows that maximum use should be made of available power. This leads to the need for some standard for transmitter efficiency. This does not mean that a simple specification of efficiency based upon power delivered to a 50-ohm load would be appropriate, because few of these devices are designed to work into 50 ohms. It would be desireable to develop some criteria whereby a high level of efficiency could be assured, thereby providing the maximum signal strength and transmitting time consistent with the battery power available.

A second component of a standard should be a specification of operating frequencies. This would include a safeguard against the use of transmitters operating in the aircraft landing system bands, which could constitute a very serious hazard to air travel. A serious accident caused by an electronic surveillance system operating on instrument landing system frequencies is too high a price to pay for any evidence which might be thus obtained. The exclusion of these frequencies would eliminate the use of the detuned commercial FM receiver as a listening post, and require the purchase of receivers manufactured specifically for surveillance work. Although this is an economic penalty, it will likely pay off handsomely in terms of system performance because many commercial FM undercover receivers are of relatively poor quality.

Finally, the modulation bandwidths characteristic of high-fidelity equipment are not required for good quality voice communication. Therefore, the standard can afford to relax some of the requirements normally made of equipment used, for example, in the entertainment industry.

The need for high quality training for those engaged in electronic surveillance work is most evident. This work encompasses a large body of knowledge, much of which is not to be found in textbooks and which can therefore be conveyed only by those with experience.

Much additional work is needed in the area of antenna design and evaluation, especially by body-mounted antennas where large variations in received signal strength are observable.

WIRETAPPING

Telephone Tapping Transmitters

There are several types of telephone tapping transmitters usable for monitoring both sides of a telephone conversation. In general, they are not crystal controlled and have a power output ranging from a few milliwatts to perhaps one-quarter watt; many of them use the telephone line as an antenna. All types may be located either by their radiated signal or by visual inspection. The poorer ones may be found by the current they draw from the telephone lines. If the current drain is sufficient, it can give an indication of trouble on the line and draw the attention of the telephone company repair facilities. Some difficult problems are encountered in evaluating the power output of telephone tapping transmitters. Because of the antenna arrangements they use, it is not feasible to make output power measurements into a 50 ohm load, and it becomes necessary to rely on field strength measurements to determine radiated power.

The Drop-In Telephone Transmitter

This device looks very much like the mouthpiece unit of a telephone. The carbon microphone mouthpiece drops out easily if the retaining ring over the mouthpiece is unscrewed. The drop-in transmitter may be substituted in its place very quickly and the telephone returned to apparently normal operation. The telephone transmitter draws its power from the telephone line and operates only when the receiver is lifted from the cradle. Both sides of the telephone conversation modulate the rf carrier frequency of the telephone transmitter which may be received and recorded from a remote location. One of the main advantages of the device is that it takes only a few seconds to install, and the better ones are so cleverly constructed that they may be difficult to recognize by anyone who is not extremely familiar with the telephone equipment. The drop-in transmitter does not require a separate antenna but instead uses the telephone line for this purpose. However, it is possible to detect the use of this type of transmitter by means of impedance measurements or by measuring the current drain while the telephone is in use.

The Series-Connected Telephone Transmitter

Any accessible location on the telephone line to be tapped, such as a terminal block, may be used as an installation point for a series connected transmitter. Therefore, direct access to the telephone instrument is not required. The circuit in Figure 1 illustrates the method of connection. The polarity is not important, so the transmitter may be installed in either side of the line. Because series-connected transmitters draw current from the telephone line, they can be detected in the same manner as drop-in transmitters.

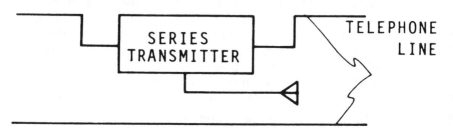

Figure 1. Series-connected telephone transmitter.

The Parallel-Connected Telephone Transmitter

Figure 2 illustrates the method used to connect a parallel transmitter to a telephone line. Again, the polarity is usually not important, but there are several differences between this installation and the series transmitter. Because the parallel transmitter is powered by a separate battery, it draws no current from the phone line and is essentially undetectable by impedance or current measurement techniques. As with any battery-powered device, it has a limited operating time. The transmitter is activated whenever the receiver is lifted.

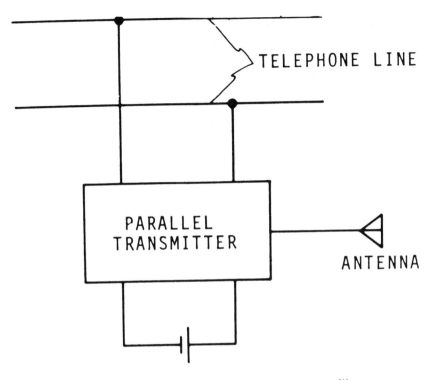

Figure 2. Parallel-connected telephone transmitter.

Telephone Taps

Surveillance must often be carried out by using remotely located tape recording equipment to record the telephone conversations. The fact that telephone companies install extra wiring in anticipation of future demands for service provides a unique and convenient situation for wiretapping. Almost invariably, there will be one or more pairs of conductors in a cable which are not in use and which can be appropriated for surveillance purposes. These pairs are easily located at various access points in a given building or neighborhood by someone who is familiar with the telephone system and its equipment. Thus, not only the telephone itself but the whole wire communication network offers a limitless range of possibilities to the skillful technician. Even if a thorough examination were to determine that the telephone itself was not being tapped, there would still be no guarantee that a hidden microphone was not present which was carrying the conversation within a room to a remote listening post via telephone wiring. In the following paragraphs, some of the more frequently used telephone tapping methods and equipment are discussed along with the methods used to detect them.

"Infinity Transmitter" or "Harmonica Bug"

Although the infinity transmitter is installed in the telephone, it does not monitor telephone conversations. Instead, it enables someone to listen in on a room conversation by means of another telephone. Once the device is installed in a telephone, a listener dials the number of the altered telephone in the customary manner. However, just before the dialed telephone rings, an audible noise or tone is transmitted over the phone line. This activates the bug, which opens the phone line without ringing, thereby enabling the caller to listen to any conversation taking place in the vicinity of the bugged telephone. The bug itself is an electronic switch which closes in response to the audio tone. It is wired in parallel to the hookswitch on the telephone so that, upon being activated, it prevents the telephone from ringing and opens the phone line at the same time. When this bug is in operation, the telephone will be busy to all other callers even though the receiver is in the cradle in the usual position. Thus, one symptom of the presence of such a bug is the receipt of a busy signal when the phone is known not to be in use. This device must be installed in the telephone and can be located by physical search. Defensive equipment is manufactured which will place a tone sweep on the phone line and detect the voltage drop from 48 volts to approximately 8 volts when such a bug is activated. A tone sweep is necessary because these bugs can be made to respond to a wide range of audio frequencies. The name "harmonica bug" is derived from the use of a common harmonica to actuate the device.

Inductive Coupling or "Pick-Up Calls"

A current in a conductor gives rise to a magnetic field around the conductor; when the current varies either in magnitude or direction, the magnetic field also changes. Conversely, if a conductor is immersed in a changing magnetic field, a current will be produced. This is the principle of the transformer and is used as a means of tapping a telephone. Various types of coils and pick-up loops can be employed to couple to an active telephone line and hence to monitor the conversation in progress. Many such devices are used in conjunction with an audio amplifier to actuate a tape recorder or to modulate a radio transmitter. Such devices do not produce any measurable loading or draw any detectable extra current from the line and therefore can not be located by voltage or current measurements. Physical search is practically the only means of detecting such a device.

Three-Wire System

A telephone may be used for both tapping and bugging simultaneously by the use of a third conductor for bypassing the hookswitch and thereby activating the mouthpiece for use as a room bug. Telephone hookswitch bypass is the term sometimes used to refer to this method of eavesdropping and some highly sophisticated electronic devices are employed to accomplish it and to make detection difficult.

Dialed Number Recorder

Although not a device for intercepting oral communication, the dialed number recorder is used to monitor telephone calls by providing a record of all numbers dialed from a particular telephone. These devices usually provide a paper tape printout of numbers dialed, and in addition may provide the date and time the call was made. Such devices were once called "pen registers" because a pen riding on a moving chart was used. The pen records the groups of pulses emitted by the telephone dial mechanism as it returns to the rest position. The dialed number is ascertained by counting the number of pulses in each group. In telephone systems using touch-tone dialing, a touch-tone decoder with a printed readout is used. These instruments are manufactured mainly for use by the telephone companies. Application is very simple, requiring only the connection of a lead to each side of the telephone line. No legal implications are involved, and connection can be made anywhere along the line between the telephone and the exchange. Detection of the presence of a dialed number recorder is extremely difficult by any means other than visual inspection, because these devices have a high input impedance and the line loading effect is negligible.

WIRETAPPING SCENARIOS

This section outlines three examples of possible approaches to electronic surveillance communication interception. The purpose is to illustrate the types of strategies that could be employed in carrying out an electronic communications interception operation. These approaches are:

- Interception of a suburban residential telephone.
- Interception of a business's data communication to a computer service.
- Interception of conversations over the direct distance dialing network between two specific individuals in different cities.

It is necessary to make specific assumptions about the objectives of the interceptor, the characteristics of the telephone company plant and the target, and the environment within which the operation is to take place. These assumptions are stated for each case under the heading "Situation".

INTERCEPTION OF A SUBURBAN RESIDENTIAL TELEPHONE

Situation

The interceptor is interested in conversations a particular individual might have with other unknown individuals. He would also like to know the identity of the other party to the conversation of interest, if possible. The information of interest would be communicated using the targeted individual's home telephone sometime between 6 pm and 11 pm, Monday through Friday. The call could be originated by the targeted individual or by one of the unknown individuals. The residential area is similar to that found in Northern Virginia outside the Beltway. The interceptor knows the location of the home of the targeted individual.

Since the interceptor does not know the identity of the other individuals, nor who will originate the call(s) of interest, he must perform his interception on the local subscriber loop.

The local subscriber loop consists of an aerial drop wire from the house to a nearby pole-mounted terminal where it is connected to an aerial distribution cable consisting of 25 pairs. The distribution cable runs several blocks to another pole-mounted terminal where it connects to an aerial branch feeder cable consisting of 200 pairs (made up of 8 binder groups). The branch feeder cable runs several blocks to another pole-mounted terminal where it connects with an aerial main feeder cable consisting of 600 pairs (made up of 24 binder groups). All cable except the drop wire is Alpeth (consisting of polyethylene and aluminum sheath). The main branch feeder cable is pressurized. None of the terminal cases or other terminal appearances are locked or pressurized. Initially unknown to the interceptor, the only suitable place to hide his monitering station is a wooded section adjacent to the main feeder cable.

Signal Acquisition Strategy

A possible strategy for the interceptor is as follows:

1. Visually trace drop wire to the distribution terminal.

2. Climb pole, open terminal enclosure and note color code of the pair in the distribution cable to which the drop wire is attached.

3. Visually trace distribution cable to the branch feeder terminal and look for suitable place to hide monitoring station.

4. Climb pole, open terminal enclosure and note color code of the binder group containing the pair of interest. Also note if the color code of the pair of interest has changed.

5. Visually trace branch feeder cable to the main feeder cable terminal and look for suitable place to hide monitoring station.

6. Climb pole, open terminal enclosure and note color code of binder group containing the pair of interest. Also note if the color code of the pair of interest has changed.

7. Visually trace main feeder cable to suitable place for hiding monitoring station and look for the nearest appearance (assume a terminal enclosure). (Note: terminal enclosure was chosen rather than penetrating cable at a closer point because terminal enclosure is not pressurized but cable is.)

8. Open terminal enclosure and attach own wire-pair to same binding posts to which wire-pair of interest is attached.

9. If the interceptor wishes to check to see if he has the correct pair, he can remove the subscriber side of the pair of interest and attach a test set with ring generator and talk battery to subscriber pair and ring subscriber's telephone. After verification, he re-establishes the normal connection and removes the test set.

10. Run own pair to a high impedance amplifier (battery powered) which he mounts on the same or adjacent pole. Run a wire-pair along route to a pole from which the pair can be run into the wooded area with little likelihood of being discovered.
11. Attach monitoring equipment.

Monitoring Equipment and Procedure

The monitoring equipment could consist of a set of headphones, a signaling decoder and a tape recorder. The first item needs no power. The latter two would be battery powered. Two basic operational procedures are visualized: attended operation and unattended operation.

Attended Operation

The interceptor need be on site only between 6 pm and 11 pm, Monday through Friday. The interceptor would use the headphones to listen to conversations. The signaling decoder could be used to alert him to an off-hook condition so that he need not listen when telephone is not being used. It could also be used to display the telephone number of parties being called by the targeted individual. If the interceptor wishes to have a record of the conversation of interest, he can manually start the tape recorder when the off-hook condition is detected. The tape could be immediately erased if the conversation was not of interest (in order to save tape). The interceptor could take the monitoring equipment with him when he leaves the site in order to minimize chances of accidental discovery of monitoring site.

Unattended Operation

The interceptor need only be on-site for the initial setup, to change tapes and to replace batteries. The headphones would be useful when he is on-site to check the equipment operation. A timer is added to the equipment to energize the equipment at 6 pm and turn it off at 11 pm. The signaling decoder need recognize only the on-hook/off-hook condition and run the recorder only when an off-hook condition exists. Telephone numbers could be identified when tape is played back. The intercept equipment could be camouflaged (perhaps buried) in order to minimize risk of accidental detection.

INTERCEPTION OF A BUSINESS'S DATA COMMUNICATION TO A COMPUTER SERVICE

Situation

The interceptor is interested in the data exchanged between a business and a computer center (e.g., the business might have the computer center handling all their accounting). The business always originates the call to the computer center via a special telephone number (unknown to interceptor). Data is collected by a mini-computer on the premises of the business and periodically transferred to the computer service. The business can interrogate the computer service for processed information (based on its own input data). Information exchange is coded using the American Standard Code for Information Interchange (ASCII) (code used is unknown to interceptor). The modem used is a Bell 203A data set operating at 2400 bps in the half-duplex mode (unknown to interceptor). This is the only data service used by the business.

There are 20 subscriber loops terminating in a PBX. These are carried in a 25-pair aerial distribution cable which runs a short distance outside the premises of the business to a pole-mounted terminal where it is connected to a buried branch feeder cable consisting of 300 pairs (made up of 8 binder groups). Part of the branch feeder cable is laid in a trench through an easement on the property of a building which can be rented. There are no above ground appearances near the property. All cable is Alpeth and the branch feeder cable is pressurized. None of the appearances of the distribution cable are locked or pressurized.

Signal Acquisition Strategy

A possible strategy for the interceptor is as follows:

1. Visually trace distribution cable to the branch feeder terminal.

2. Climb pole, open terminal enclosure and note color code of binder group in branch feeder cable carrying 20 subscriber loops. (It is assumed that all subscriber loops are carried in one 25-pair binder group.)

3. Visually trace marked right-of-way of the buried branch feeder cable to the property which can be rented. Rent property.

4. Dig trench from building to branch feeder cable and dig up cable.

5. Install gas pressurization by-pass. (By-pass consists of a tube which is connected to cable clamps at both ends.) Drill two small holes (say 24 inches apart) in cable sheath, being careful not to damage pairs and clamp by-pass to the two holes. Cut through cable sheath at two points between the clamps and remove sheath. Plug both ends using a pressure gun filled with a quick-drying compound.

6. Separate binder groups, identify group of interest (from color code), strip insulation from each wire in the group and splice the 25 pairs to 25 voice band high-input impedance amplifiers. Attach own 25-pair cable to outputs of amplifiers and a 2-conductor power cord to a power supply for the amplifiers.

7. Assuming the interceptor knows the correct special three-digit number to dial, he can check to be sure that he has the correct binder group by attaching a standard test set to a working pair and dialing these three digits followed by the last four digits of the telephone number of the business of interest. This action results in a tone being placed on the line by the central office. The interceptor depresses his switch hook momentarily (he may

have to repeatedly depress switch hook) until the tone goes away. He hangs up. The central office sends out ringing current on the line. The PBX operator answers either with the company name or interceptor asks if he has reached the XYZ company. He makes an excuse and hangs up. (Note: the latter action must be completed quickly because some central offices place a tone on the dial after about 20 seconds to a few minutes.)

8. Lay the 25-pair cable and the power cord in the trench and fill in the trench and the hole.

9. Attach monitoring equipment and plug power cord into AC outlet.

Monitoring Equipment and Procedure

The monitoring equipment might consist of a set of headphones; a 25-input signalling decoder for recognizing on-hook/off-hook and 5 dial pulse decoders which display the numbers being called; a modem; a standard oscilloscope; a data scope; a tape recorder; a printer and an intercept equipment controller (e.g., microprocessor).

The interceptor determines the telephone number of the computer service by briefly listening to each line when it goes off-hook and noting the telephone number from the dialed pulse decoder display when he hears the distinctive sound of digital data being transmitted. He then sets the controller to recognize (via the dial pulse decoders) when the particular number of the computer service is being called and to connect the line to a pair of output jacks to which he has attached an oscilloscope. By observing the waveform of the line signal, he will be able to determine the modulation and bit rate being used. (In this case, a vestigal sideband, 2-level amplitude modulated carrier operating at 2400 bps.) If he is familiar with the line signals of standard data sets, he could obtain a 203A equivalent from a manufacturer. On the other hand, the interceptor may have on hand a general purpose demodulator with adjustments for detecting the signal. (Note: Line compensation would not be necessary because the interceptor is close enough to the data transmitter.) If the interceptor is able to identify and obtain the appropriate data set, he can proceed to the next step. If not, he must determine the transmitting modem's operations on the input data stream. (In this case, a scrambler using a 23-bit shift register followed by a Binary-to-Gray code converter.) This can be a lengthy process until the interceptor is familiar with the various types of scramblers used. (Note: This process puts a premium on the interceptor finding out ahead of time the particular modem being used.) The interceptor could defer this problem to a later time by tape recording the line signal.

In either case, after the line signal has been passed through the proper modem, the interceptor must determine the code being used for communication between the business of interest and the computer service (in this case, ASCII). This may be accomplished for standard codes with the aid of a device known as a data scope.

To recover the information of interest, the interceptor will need a printer which accepts the ASCII code and will determine the format of the data by examination of the output of the printer.

INTERCEPTION OF CONVERSATIONS OVER THE DIRECT DISTANCE DIALING NETWORK BETWEEN TWO SPECIFIC INDIVIDUALS IN DIFFERENT CITIES

Situation

The interceptor is interested in obtaining information being passed in telephone conversations between individuals located in different cities. The interceptor has been able to acquire the numbers of the telephones most likely to be used in making the calls. By studying materials available through the FCC and by physical surveillance, the interceptor has been able to establish that there are three physical routes linking the two cities (as well as other cities near the routes) and the approximate location of each. The three routes are:

- A TD-2 microwave system carrying 14,800 voice channels,
- A coaxial cable having 8 tubes with 1860 voice channels per tube for a total of 14,880 channels, and
- A pressurized multi-pair cable having 200 wire-pairs with 8 of the wire-pairs carrying 24 voice channels each and the remainder single voice channels.

Unknown to the interceptor is the fact that the high usage trunk group between the sectional center in one city and the regional center in the other consists of 36 two-way trunks. Twenty-four are routed via the radio route and twelve via the coaxial route. No trunks of the preferred high-usage trunk group are routed via the multi-pair cable route.

Signal Acquisition Strategy

The interceptor chooses to be pragmatic in his approach. He knows that the trunk group between the cities is probably divided among the routes. He also knows the difficulties of penetrating and acquiring signals for coaxial cable systems. He is aware of the high voltage hazards and the monitoring and alarm systems associated with the coaxial cable and its repeater stations. The interceptor decides he does not need to intercept every call made by the targeted individuals. Therefore, he chooses to be satisfied with whatever portion of the calls he can acquire from the radio route and the multi-pair cable and to take all the time necessary to get the information he desires.

The interceptor would then proceed to pinpoint the paths of the two routes selected by searching out the repeater huts, repeater manholes, cable markers, micro-wave towers and other indications of rights-of-way. The basic geography of the radio route could be easily determined from FCC filings which are available to the public (and can be subscribed to at nominal cost). An alternative way of determining the radio path would be to simply observe the azimuthal orientation of the antennas on the central office roof and extrapolate the azimuths radiating from the central office location on a suitable map to their destination.

The interceptor's next steps are to acquire telephone main stations connected with the exchanges to which the targeted telephones are connected and to recruit accomplices. The interceptor would employ several crews to search out the routes, set up interception stations, find the trunk circuits and target desired communications.

The general strategy for finding the trunk circuits is to have accomplices place calls between telephones connected to the targeted central office switching machines, place easily identifiable tracer signals on the line such as tones, and to scan the trunk circuits at the interception sites until the tracer signals are located. The interception sites would then notify the callers that the tone has been found. The callers and interception site personnel would then repeat the process a number of times throughout the day, sampling the circuits during times of both high and low usage in order to estimate the portion of the high usage trunk group that is assigned to each of the media routed between the exchanges of interest. The specific acquisition activities for the radio and multi-pair cable routes are described below.

Microwave Radio Signal Acquisition

A possible strategy for intercepting the calls on the radio route is as follows:

1. Locate the microwave repeater sites for the route of interest either through physical observation or from FCC filings.

2. Acquire the use of a small farm along the route with sufficient line-of-site access to the radiated energy.

3. Set up radio interception equipment including a sufficiently large antenna in a barn to avoid being observed.

4. Place call between accomplices and put tracer signals on the circuit.

5. Scan the microwave channels to find tracer signals.

6. Telephone accomplice from farm either when tracer is found or no tracer tone can be found (accomplice must have second main station telephone to receive such a call) and have him end call and place a new call with the tracer tone.

7. Begin monitoring the channels on which tracer signals were found.

8. Continue search for trunk circuits until the portion of the trunk group carried by the microwave route has been approximately identified.

9. Terminate use of tracer calls and continue to monitor the circuits for desired information.

10. Program microcomputer equipped with inband signaling decode device to automatically scan the groups of interest. In the event either of the two targeted telephones is dialed, the scanning device will either signal the interceptor to listen, or automatically connect a recorder to the conversation.

11. Recorded conversations can either be analyzed for relevant communications in situ or transported to an information extraction facility.

Multi-Pair Cable Signal Acquisition

A possible strategy for the interceptor is as follows:

1. Trace cable route between cities by means of process discussed above. Find suitable site along cable path either in an isolated area, or on a rental property, where the interception station can be concealed.

2. Dig trench from interception station to cable and dig up cable. Upon finding cable to be pressurized, install a gas pressurization bypass, plug

cable, and penetrate sheath as described in the previous example.

3. Splice in 22 pair cable which connects to high impedance amplifier inputs at the interception station. (If the cable run is longer than 300 feet, the high impedance amplifiers will have to be located at the cable or an intermediate point and powered from the interception station.) Bury the splice point and cable trench.

4. Examine all pairs to determine which pairs carry single voice conversations and which carry multiplex systems. Attach either voice-band monitoring equipment or demultiplexing receivers to the pairs according to the types of system found.

5. Utilize the tracer signal process discussed above to find desired trunk circuits carried by the cable. For wire-pairs carrying single voice conversations, signal back to the accomplices over the wire that the tracer signal had or had not been detected and a new call should be placed. For circuits carrying multiplexed channels, telephone the accomplice. (If the interception site is in a remote location, the communication to the accomplice would probably need to be relayed by radio (e.g., CB Radio) to another accomplice having access to a telephone.)

6. After sufficient testing, the interceptor concludes that none of the trunk circuits of interest are routed on the multi-pair cable and concentrates his efforts on getting the desired information from the microwave system.

Monitoring Equipment and Procedure

Most of the equipment will be required for monitoring the microwave radio route. In addition to receiver-demultiplexer (which also is used on multi-pair cable route), a radio receiver and antenna system are required. A moderate amount of knowledge and expertise would be required to analyze the radio path, find and install the interception site, and utilize the interception equipment, but the risk of being discovered is fairly low.

The multi-pair cable route requires special tools to dig up the cable and dig a trench to an interception shelter, as well as the cable to interconnect the penetration point with the shelter. The shelter might be a farm house, van or some form of temporary shelter. Special tools and skills will also be required to penetrate the cable, spoof the gas pressurization system, and strip/splice the individual cable pairs. The multi-pair cable interception equipment, if intentionally minimized, could be the least costly of all. Of course, in this example, the desired signals were not on the multi-pair cable.

TELEPHONE BUGGING

Many people consider the possibility that their telephone conversations may be monitored. Most do not consider that what they say after the telephone is hung-up may be overheard also by the same telephone instrument. Frequently, what is said immediately after a telephone conversation is far more interesting than what was said during the telephone conversation. It is, of course, an obvious fact that bugging can be accomplished by other means (wired microphone, radio transmitter, power-line carrier, etc.). There are, however, several reasons why the telephone is preferable as a listening device to other bugging techniques. One of the most important is that the telephone, with its three existing microphones (carbon microphone, dynamic earphone, and microphonic ringer) is usually at an optimum location for pick-up of conversations taking place in the room. This is particularly true in an office with the telephone on the desk. Because the microphones are inherent to the telephone, there are no concealment requirements. While these microphones require conductors to carry the acquired audio to a listening post, again no concealment is involved. The telephone system provides the conductors. Another advantage is that no power is required in the target area, since the power used is either telephone system power or can be provided from the listening post; no battery replacement problems exist. This system does not radiate, so it will not be inadvertently discovered by a nearby receiver. The listening post may be anywhere between the telephone instrument and the exchange. Lastly, most telephone bugging techniques also provide both sides of the conversations without extra installation of equipment.

There are several ways in which telephone bugs can be categorized. Perhaps the most simple is the three ways in which the microphone is connected to the listening post.

The first of these is *Direct Connection* by means of the telephone lines. The second is *Third-Wire* or *Spare-Pair*, where the additional conductor(s) are used to complete the circuit on the handset side of the hookswitch. The third is *Hookswitch Bypass*, with which the normally open hookswitch is caused to appear closed for eavesdropping purposes.

Direct Connection

A microphonic ringer constitutes a directly connected microphone. A separate microphone could be added to the telephone on the exchange side of the hookswitch, provided it were DC blocked and did not reduce the telephone conversation audio. Other techniques, which will be discussed under hookswitch bypass, could be used, but since they would require an additional microphone when microphones are available on the other side of the hookswitch, they are unlikely. In the case of the ringer, detection is not a problem, since we know it is there. The problem is to determine whether it is sufficiently microphonic to cause a hazard. This is most effectively accomplished by a listening test. Other techniques, unlikely though they may be, will be detected by the techniques used to detect hookswitch bypasses.

Third-Wire or Spare-Pair

This technique allows direct connection to either the dynamic earphone or the carbon microphone by using the spare conductor(s) in the mounting cord. In years past, this was the prevalent telephone bugging technique. It is seldom used today because it requires equally spare conductors between those in the mounting cord and the listening post. The running of additional conductors negates some of the advantages of telephone bugging. Also, it is detectable by a simple ohmmeter test to determine whether the spare conductor(s) measure other than a short circuit or an open circuit between themselves or either of the other two conductors. Either the dynamic earphone or the carbon microphone may be used with this technique. The dynamic earphone requires that the shorting contacts be disabled, as previously discussed. No external power is required with the dynamic earphone; however, the output is low and the resultant signal-to-noise ratio, considered against cross-talk and line noise in the telephone, is not nearly as good as the carbon microphone powered from the listening post.

Hookswitch Bypass

Hookswitch bypass involves completing the connection across the hookswitch(es) in such a manner that the exchange is not alerted. Again, either the dynamic earphone or the carbon microphone can be used as the eavesdropping microphone. The same requirements for power to the carbon microphone exist, and the signal-to-noise problems with the dynamic earphone are worse, since the exchange lines are used directly and the cross-talk and line noises are much greater. There are a number of methods of bypassing the hookswitch, with varying degrees of security against detection, signal-to-noise ratio, and convenience. Normally, only one hookswitch is bypassed. If the telephone has two, the second is usually shorted. While the bypasses will be discussed as if they were connected directly across the open hookswitch terminals, in most cases effort will be made to conceal them.

Capacitance Bypass

Of the hookswitch bypasses, the capacitance bypass is the only one which is used with the dynamic earphone. The capacitor bridges the unshorted hookswitch, blocks the DC voltage from the exchange, and passes the audio from the dynamic earphone. For the reasons mentioned above, this is the least effective type of bypass. This bypass can be detected with an amplifier, in the same manner as the microphonic ringer. It can be detected also with capacitance detection techniques. Typical values of capacitance are .01 to .001 microfarads.

Resistance Bypass

This bypass allows DC current to flow through the carbon microphone, but limits the current to a value below that which will activate the exchange. A normal value for this resistor is 10,000 ohms. This will limit the current flow to about 5 milliamperes, when exchange voltage is used to provide the current. This bypass degrades the audio signal as it reduces the current flow. It can be detected with an ohm-meter.

Resistance-Capacitance (RC) Bypass

This bypass is similar to the Resistance Bypass, above, except the resistor is paralleled with a capacitor to enhance the audio signal. This bypass is effective, but it can be detected with an ohm-meter.

Reversed-Bias Diode

This bypass consists of a diode placed across the hookswitch in blocking polarity. In this polarity, the diode appears as an open circuit and has no effect on the telephone. To activate the bypass, the telephone line polarity is reversed. If the exchange voltage is to be used, a resistor of 5,000 to 10,000 ohms must be placed in series with the diode to prevent engaging the exchange. A more effective technique involves opening the lines to the exchange and providing the reversed polarity voltage from a separate source at the listening post. Provisions must be made to instantly restore the exchange lines if there is an incoming call or the handset is lifted for an outgoing call. Automatic switches are used for this purpose. This is a very effective technique, but it can be detected by an ohm-meter, if resistance readings are taken in both polarities. This is the first technique described that can be turned on and off by the eavesdropper to help prevent its detection by listening on the phone lines after working hours, when most countermeasures inspections are made.

Neon-Tube Bypass

This bypass is the first of the voltage-fired devices to be used as a bypass. These devices are used for greater security against detection. They can be turned on and off from the listening post and they can not be detected by amplifier test or ohm-meter test — the usual detection techniques. The neon-tube (neon-lamp) requires approximately 65 volts DC to cause it to fire. Since the exchange voltage is no more than 50 volts, the neon around the hookswitch constitutes an open circuit until the voltage across it is raised and held at or above its firing voltage. Once it is in conduction, it behaves like a closed switch. The firing potential is provided from the listening post. The telephone lines between the listening post and the exchange must be either opened or diode blocked to prevent the exchange from being a part of the higher voltage circuit. The neon-tube bypass tends to be noisy, partly because the current flow through the neon must be limited to about 3 milliamperes. Security can be increased by stacking neons in series so that the firing voltage required to fire them is a multiple of the nominal 65 volts. Since the firing voltage must be sustained to keep the neons in conduction, there is a practical limit to the number of neons which may be stacked realistically. Voltages over 500 volts may break down the ringer capacitor. This limits the number of neons which may be stacked to a practical seven. Stacking the neons tends to increase the noise. Detection must be by voltage breakdown.

Diode-Blocked Zener

Similar to the neon-tube, the zener diode has a voltage threshold level below which it does not conduct; however, this characteristic is polarity sensitive. When the polarity is reversed, it behaves like a normal diode and conducts freely. A high-voltage diode is used to block this free conduction so that the array conducts only when the firing voltage polarity is correct, and then only when the proper firing voltage (equal to or greater than) is applied. This bypass allows more current to be used than does the neon, provided a sufficiently high wattage zener is selected. Zeners can be smaller than neons, and zeners are available in a variety of voltages.

Other than these stated differences, the information about neons applies.

Four-Layer Bypass

The ultimate in hookswitch bypass is the four-layer device. This is a solid-state switch which once switched will remain on as long as minimum current flow (called Holding Current) exists. It is turned off by causing the current flow to stop momentarily. There are commercially available three types of four-layer devices: the four-layer diode; the silicon controlled rectifier (SCR); and the TRIAC. The four-layer diode has two terminals; the SCR and TRIAC have three. The four-layer diode is fired by pulsing across its terminal with a short duration pulse which meets or exceeds its firing voltage requirements. Unlike the neon or zener, the firing voltage need not be sustained; a very low voltage will suffice, provided the holding current requirements continue to be met. The SCR and TRIAC operate in the same manner; additionally, the SCR and TRIAC have a second turn-on means — a gate electrode which requires only a low voltage to produce switching. The SCR is unidirectional; the TRIAC is bi-directional. Four-layer devices are available with firing voltages ranging from a few volts to 800 volts. These devices may be stacked to increase the firing voltage requirements. The number which may be stacked is not limited by the telephone, as is the case with neons and zeners, since the high-voltage pulse may be severely current-limited and need be only microseconds long. Once switched, the holding current source takes over. The limitation on the eavesdropper is line-capacitance, which tends to degrade his high-voltage pulse. The further he is from the telephone instrument, the greater his problem. In demonstrations of this Telephone Analyzer, we have fired stacks of 13 devices, each requiring in excess of 400 volts. Since we are working directly into the detached telephone, we have an advantage over the eavesdropper. It must be assumed, however, that the eavesdropper is capable of using stacks requiring 3,000 to 3,500 volts firing voltage. In addition to being available in normal configuration, these devices are available in chips measuring 0.1" x 0.1" x .003", which makes them very concealable. An additional modification is the turn-on delay, which is accomplished by paralleling the four-layer device with a capacitor and placing a resistor in series with it. This requires that the firing voltage be sustained for the period of the delay established by the Resistance/Capacitance circuit. Four-layer bypasses are detected by voltage breakdown. Delayed turn-on devices are detected by components used to form the delay.

Infinity Transmitter

The infinity transmitter, also called the *harmonica bug*, can be used as a hookswitch bypass. This device is basically a tone-activated switch. When installed in the telephone it fulfills the same function as any controllable hookswitch bypass (i.e., it connects the carbon microphone to the outgoing lines around the hookswitch upon receipt of a signal). The infinity transmitter allows the eavesdropper to transmit the signal and activate the bypass from any direct-dial phone in the world. After planting the device, the eavesdropper can dial the number of the target telephone and must immediately feed his tone signal into the mouthpiece from the telephone from which he is calling. When the call reaches the exchange of the target telephone and the incoming call is switched to the target telephone, before the ring signal has been initiated, the tone signal is received by the infinity transmitter, which switches and, in effect, answers the call. Once this occurs, the ring signal is inhibited, so the ring never occurs. (This is not the case with German telephone systems.) From this time until the infinity transmitter is turned off, the eavesdropper listens to the room conversations.

Although we were concerned with other hookswitch bypass systems, so much current would flow that the exchange would be activated, in this case, we must assure that sufficient current flows to activate the exchange and hold it in that state. The infinity transmitter poses one operational problem. For the entire period that the eavesdropper is listening, the target telephone is actually in use and will indicate busy to any other incoming call.

The same telephone instrument tests that will detect the other hookswitches will detect the infinity transmitter. If the transmitter is activated, on-line voltage tests will definitely detect it, since the on-line voltage will be at least 10 volts lower than normal hung-up voltage. Additionally, a slow tone sweep applied to the telephone lines will activate it. The last two tests are valid, even if the infinity transmitter is connected to the telephone lines outside the telephone (with its own microphone).

APPLICABLE LAWS

This chapter reprints in whole applicable Federal laws pertaining to wiretapping and electronic eavesdropping.

18§2510

Definitions

As used in this chapter:

(1) "wire communication" means any communication made in whole or in part through the use of facilities for the transmission of communications by the aid of wire, cable or other like connection between the point of origin and the point of reception furnished or operated by any person engaged as a common carrier in providing or operating such facilities for the transmission of interstate or foreign communication;

(2) "oral communication" means any oral communication uttered by a person exhibiting an expectation that such communication is not subject to interception under circumstances justifying such expectation;

(3) "State" means any State of the United States, the District of Columbia, the Commonwealth of Puerto Rico, and any territory or possession of the United States;

(4) "intercept" means the aural acquisition of the contents of any wire or oral communication through the use of any electronic, mechanical or other device;

(5) "electronic, mechanical or other device" means any device or apparatus which can be used to intercept a wire or oral communication other than:

(a) any telephone or telegraph instrument, equipment or facility, or any component thereof, (i) furnished to the subscriber or user by a communications common carrier in the ordinary course of its business and being used by the subscriber or user in the ordinary course of its business; or (ii) being used by a communications common carrier in the ordinary course of its business, or by an investigative or law enforcement officer in the ordinary course of his duties.

(b) a hearing aid or similar device being used to correct subnormal hearing to not better than normal;

(6) "person" means any employee, or agent of the United States or any State or political subdivision thereof, and any individual, partnership, association, joint stock company, trust, or corporation;

(7) "investigative or law enforcement officer" means any officer of the United States or of a State or political subdivision thereof, who is empowered by law to conduct investigations or to make arrests for offenses enumerated in this chapter, and any attorney authorized by law to prosecute or participate in the prosecution of such offenses;

(8) "contents", when used with respect to any wire or oral communication, includes any information concerning the identity of the parties to such communication or the existence, substance, purport, or meaning of that communication;

(9) "judge of competent jurisdiction" means:

(a) a judge of a United States district court or a United States court of appeals; and

(b) a judge of any court of general criminal jurisdiction of a State who is authorized by a statute of the State to enter orders authorizing interceptions of wire or oral communications;

(10) "communication common carrier" shall have the same meaning which is given the term "common carrier" by section 153(h) of title 47 of the United States Code; and

(11) "aggrieved person" means a person who was a party to any intercepted wire or oral communication or a person against whom the interception was directed.

Added Pub.L. 90-351, Title III, §802, June 19, 1968, §2 Stat. 112.

18§2511

Interception and disclosure of wire or oral communication prohibited

(1) Except as otherwise specifically provided in this chapter, any person who:

(a) Willfully intercepts, endeavors to intercept, or procures any other person to intercept or endeavor to intercept, any wire or oral communication;

(b) willfully uses, endeavors to use, or procures any other person to use or endeavor to use any electronic, mechanical, or other device to intercept any oral communication when:

(i) such device is affixed to, or otherwise transmits a signal through a wire, cable, or other like connection used in wire communication; or

(ii) such device transmits communications by radio, or interferes with the transmission of such communication; or

(iii) such person knows, or has reason to know, that such device or any component thereof has been sent through the mail or transported in interstate or foreign commerce; or

(iv) such use or endeavor to use (A) takes place on the premises of any business or other commercial establishment the operations of which affect interstate or foreign commerce; or (B) obtains or is for the purpose of obtaining information relating to the operations of any business or other commercial establishment the operations of which affect interstate or foreign commerce; or

(v) such persons act in the District of Columbia, the Commonwealth of Puerto Rico, or any territory or possession of the United States;

(c) willfully discloses, or endeavors to disclose, to any other persons the contents of any wire or oral communication, knowing or having reason to know that the information was obtained through the interception of a wire or oral communication in violation of this subsection; or

(d) willfully uses, or endeavors to use, the contents of any wire or oral communication, knowing or having reason to know that the information was obtained through the interception of a wire or oral communication in violation of this subsection;

shall be fined not more than $10,000 or imprisoned not more than five years, or both.

(2)(a)(i) It shall not be unlawful under this chapter for an operator of a switchboard, or an officer, employee, or agent of any communication common carrier, whose facilities are used in the transmission of a wire communication, to intercept, disclose, or use that communication in the normal course of his employment while engaged in any activity which is a necessary incident to the rendition of his service or to the protection of the rights or property of the carrier of such communication: Provided, That said communication common carriers shall not utilize service observing or random monitoring except for mechanical or service quality control checks.

(ii) It shall not be unlawful under this chapter for an officer, employee or agent of any communication common carrier to provide information, facilities, or technical assistance to an investigative or law enforcement officer who, pursuant to this chapter, is authorized to intercept a wire or oral communication.

(b) It shall not be unlawful under this chapter for an officer, employee or agent of the Federal Communications Commission, in the normal course of his employment and in discharge of the monitoring responsibilities exercised by the Commission in the enforcement of chapter 5 of title 47 of the United States Code, to intercept a wire communication, or oral communication transmitted by radio, or to disclose the information thereby obtained.

(c) It shall not be unlawful under this chapter for a person acting under color of law to intercept a wire or oral communication, where such a person is a party to the communication or one of the parties to the communication has given prior consent to such interception.

(d) It shall not be unlawful under this chapter for a person not acting under color of law to intercept wire or oral communication where such a person is a party to the communication or where one of the parties to the communication has given prior consent to such interception unless such communication is intercepted for the purpose of committing any criminal or tortious act in violation of the Constitution or laws of the United States of of any State or for the purpose of committing any other injurious act.

(3) Nothing contained in this chapter or in section 605 of the Communications Act of 1934 (48 Stat. 1143; 47 U.S.C. 605) shall limit the constitutional power of the President to take such measures as he deems necessary to protect the nation against actual or potential attack or other hostile acts of a foreign power, to obtain foreign intelligence information deemed essential to the security of the United States, or to protect national security information against foreign intelligence activities. Nor shall anything contained in this chapter be deemed to limit the constitutional power of the President to take such measures as he deems necessary to protect the United States against overthrow of the Government by force or other unlawful means, or against any other clear and present danger to the structure or existence of the Government. The contents of any wire or oral communication intercepted by authority of the President in the exercise of the foregoing powers may be received in evidence in any trial hearing, or other proceeding only where such interception was reasonable, and shall not be otherwise used or disclosed except as is necessary to implement that power.

Added Pub.L. 90-351, Title III, §802, June 19, 1968, 82 Stat. 213.

18§2512

Manufacture, distribution, possession, and advertising of wire or oral communication intercepting devices prohibited

(1) Except as otherwise specifically provided in this chapter, any person who willfully:

    (a) sends through the mail, or sends or carries in interstate or foreign commerce, any electronic, mechanical or other device, knowing or having reason to know that the design of such device renders it primarily useful for the purpose of the surreptitious interception of wire or oral communications;

(b) manufactures, assembles, possesses, or sells any electronic, mechanical or other device, knowing or having reason to know that the design of such device renders it primarily useful for the purpose of the surreptitious interception of wire or oral communications, and that such device or any component thereof has been or will be sent through the mail or transported in interstate or foreign commerce; or

(c) places in any newspaper, magazine, handbill, or other publication any advertisement of:

(i) any electronic, mechanical or other device knowing or having reason to know that the design of such device renders it primarily useful for the purpose of the surreptitious interception of wire or oral communications; or

(ii) any other electronic, mechanical or other device where such advertisement promotes the use of such device for the purpose of the surreptitious interception of wire or oral communications,

knowing or having reason to know that such advertisement will be sent through the mail or transported in interstate or foreign commerce,

shall be fined not more than $10,000 or imprisoned not more than five years, or both.

(2) It shall not be unlawful under this section for:

(a) a communications common carrier or an officer, agent or employee of, or a person under contract with, a communications common carrier, in the normal course of the communications common carrier's business, or

(b) an officer, agent, or employee of, or a person under contract with, the United States, a State, or a political subdivision thereof, to send through the mail, send or carry in interstate or foreign commerce, or manufacture, assemble, possess, or sell any electronic, mechanical or other device knowing or having reason to know that the design of such device renders it primarily useful for the purpose of surreptitious interception of wire or oral communications.

Added Pub.L. 90-351, Title III, §802, June 19, 1968, 82 Stat. 214.

WIRE OR RADIO COMMUNICATION
47§605

605. Unauthorized publication or use of communications

Except as authorized by chapter 119, Title 18, no person receiving, assisting in receiving, transmitting, or assisting in transmitting, any interstate or foreign communication by wire or radio, shall divulge or publish the existence, contents, substance, purport, effect, or meaning thereof, except through authorized channels of transmission or reception, (1) to any person other than the addressee, his agent, or attorney, (2) to a person employed or authorized to forward such communication to its destination, (3) to proper accounting or distributing officers of the various communicating centers over which the communication may be passed, (4) to the master of a ship under whom he is serving, (5) in response to a subpena issued by a court of competent jurisdiction, or (6) on demand of other lawful authority. No person not being authorized by the sender shall intercept any radio communication and divulge or publish the existence, contents, substance, purport, effect, or meaning of such intercepted communication to any person. No person not being entitled thereto shall receive or assist in receiving any interstate or foreign communication by radio and use such communication (or any information therein contained) for his own benefit or for the benefit of another not entitled thereto. No person having received any intercepted radio communication or having become acquainted with its contents, substance, purport, effect, or meaning of such communication (or any part thereof) knowing that such communication was intercepted, shall divulge or publish the existence, contents, substance, purport, effect or meaning of such communication (or any part thereof) or use such communication (or any information therein contained) for his own benefit or for the benefit of another not entitled thereto. This section shall not apply to the receiving, divulging, publishing or utilizing the contents of any radio communication which is broadcast or transmitted by amateurs or others for the use of the general public, or which relates to ships in distress.

As amended June 19, 1968, Pub.L. 90-351, Title III, §803 §2 Stat. 223.

ANNOTATED BIBLIOGRAPHY OF SURVEILLANCE BOOKS

For more information on covert surveillance and electronic penetration, the reader should consult the following works.

Acoustical Engineering, by H.F. Olson. D. Van Nostrand Company, Inc., Princeton, NJ, 1957. *This book contains a very detailed chapter covering microphones. This book also has an excellent chapter on recording.*

Applied Surveillance Photography, by Raymond P. Siljander. Charles C, Thomas, Publisher, Springfield, IL, 1975. *Addressed primarily to law enforcement officers, investigative and security personnel. Both still and motion picture photography are discussed. A chapter on night photography using infrared methods, and one on night photography using starlight scopes are included.*

Big Brother Game, The, by Scott French. Lyle Stuart, Secaucus, NJ, 1975. *Popular picture book on bugging, wiretapping, tailing, optical and electronic surveillance, and surreptitious entry. Lightweight, but still useful.*

Business Intelligence and Espionage, edited by R.M. Greene, Jr., Dow-Jones-Irwin, Inc., Homewood, IL, 1966. *Chapter 11 of this book is entitled "Electronic Eavesdropping (Bugging): Its Use and Countermeasures." It is a non-technical discussion of both radiating and wired devices used in undercover information-gathering activities.*

CIA Flaps and Seals Manual, edited by John M. Harrison, Paladin Press, Boulder, CO, 1975. *Tells how to open mail, and reseal it. Dry openings, wet openings, steam openings, wax seals, and much more.*

Code Book, The, by Michael E. Marotta. Loompanics Unlimited, Port Townsend, WA, 1983. *Many intercepted transmissions will be in code. This is the best introductory book on codes, codemaking and codebreaking.*

Countering Industrial Espionage, by Peter Heims. 20th Century Education, Leatherhead, Surrey, England, 1982. *Large book on industrial spying and how to counter it. Covers many electronic surveillance devices and techniques.*

Eavesdroppers, The, by D. Dash, R.F. Schwartz and R.E. Knowlton. Rutgers University Press, New Brunswick, NY, 1959. *This is a lengthy book written in three parts, namely: the practice, the tools, and the law as they pertain to eavesdropping. Because the book was written prior to the advent of miniaturized electronics, it does not deal with radiating equipment.*

Electronic Communication, second edition, by R.L. Shrader. McGraw-Hill Book Company, New York. *This book incorporates an electronics and radio communications theory course intended to prepare the reader for examinations required to obtain amateur and commercial FCC radio licenses. A great deal of the material is relevant to electronic surveillance. The book contains an excellent chapter on antennas, including a good discussion of the propagation of radio energy.*

Electronic Invasion, The, by R.M. Brown. John F. Rider Publishing, Inc., New York, 1967. *This book deals with the many types of applications of devices usable for eavesdropping, as well as those used to detect the presence of such devices. The book is written in a popularized style and contains a great deal of general information along with some technical information, including circuit diagrams.*

Electronic Measurements and Instrumentation, Volume 12 of Inter-University Electronics Series, edited by B.M. Oliver and J.M. Cage. McGraw-Hill Book Company, New

York, 1971. *This is a comprehensive book on the theory and techniques of a very wide variety of electrical and electronic measurements. Of particular importance is chapter 14, which deals with measurements on transmitters and receivers.*

Electronic Spying, by Mentor Publications. Mentor Publications, Flushing, NY, 1976. *An excellent layman's text covering all types of electronic eavesdropping, with many photos and illustrations.*

Fundamentals of Physical Surveillance, by Raymond P. Siljander. Charles C. Thomas, Publisher, Springfield, IL, 1977. *Written for police officers, this is one of the finest manuals ever produced on the subject. Included are all types of surveillance: foot, automobile, stationary and undercover.*

How to Avoid Electronic Eavesdropping and Privacy Invasion, by William W. Turner. Paladin Press, Boulder, CO, 1983. *Book by ex-FBI agent, detailing many types of transmitters, bugging devices, etc., and how to detect them.*

How to Get Anything on Anybody, by Lee Lapin. Auburn Wolfe Publishing, San Francisco, 1983. *Heavily hyped, overpriced, popular picture book, with chapters on surveillance techniques and eavesdropping.*

How to Read Lips, by Edward B. Nitchie. Hawthorne Books, Inc., New York, 1979. *Lip reading is a relevant skill for all surveillance operatives.*

How to Read Schematic Diagrams, Third Edition, by Donald E. Herrington. Howard W. Sams & Co., Inc., Indianapolis, IN, 1975. *A good introductory book on reading schematic diagrams. Written primarily for the hobbyist and beginner, it contains much information of value to the engineer and technician.*

Introduction to Acoustics, An, by R.H. Randall. Addison-Wesley Press, Inc., Cambridge, MA, 1951. *This is a college text that provides a discussion of various types of microphones, including carbon, capacitor, electrodynamic, and crystal types, and gives a comparison of their relative sensitivities.*

Methods of Electronic Audio Surveillance, by D.A. Pollack. Charles C Thomas, Publisher, Springfield, IL, 1973. *This book is an electronics manual for detectives. It is a virtual "bible" of techniques and equipment. The section on operational techniques is particularly explicit in the explanations it gives for installing room bugs and telephone taps of various kinds.*

Portfolio of Schematic Diagrams for Electronic Surveillance Devices, Mentor Publications, Flushing, NY, 1979. *A portfolio of schematic diagrams for more than two dozen electronic surveillance devices, including automobile tracking transmitters, bugging transmitters, telephone transmitters, and more.*

Techniques of Observation and Learning Retention, by Louis F. Basinger. Charles C. Thomas, Publisher, Springfield, IL, 1973. *A text for police officers to train them in the techniques of efficient observation and learning retention. These techniques are particularly adaptable to the work of field policemen, especially in the area of surveillance.*

Undercover, by Carmen J. Motto. Charles C. Thomas, Publisher, Springfield, IL, 1971. *An anecdotal book on the author's years of experience in undercover police work.*

Undercover Investigation, by J. Kirk Barefoot. Charles C. Thomas, Publisher, Springfield, IL, 1975. *This book is a blueprint for the police or military commander, or the private security person using undercover programs. Complete coverage of selecting and training personnel, establishing covers, and infiltration is given.*

Undercover Operations. Interservice Publishing Co., Inc., San Francisco, 1981. *Reprint of a military manual on selecting and training undercover operatives.*

Undercover Operations and Persuasion, by Randolph D. Hicks II. Charles C. Thomas, Publisher, Springfield, IL, 1973. *A police manual on undercover operations, centering on the use of persuasion techniques for obtaining information from suspects and protecting the safety of the officer.*

Wiretapping and Electronic Surveillance: Commission Studies. Loompanics Unlimited, Port Townsend, WA, 1983. *Reprint of government manual on state-of-the-art electronic surveillance. An excellent book on the subject. Includes methods of determining if audio tapes have been altered.*

YOU WILL ALSO WANT TO READ:

☐ **55083 Espionage: Down & Dirty,** *by Tony Lesce.* What's spying really like? Read this book and find out. Covers recruiting, training, infiltration, payment (including sex), evacuation, what happens when a spy is exposed, and more. Also reveals the exploits of many notorious spies: The Walker Spy Ring, "Falcon and Snowman," the Pollard Case, and many others. *1991, 5½ x 8½, 180 pp, soft cover.* **$17.95.**

☐ **61139 Methods of Disguise, Second Edition,** *by John Sample.* Here is an incredible, completely illustrated book on how to disguise yourself! Covers everything from "quick-change" methods to long-term, permanent disguises. Includes: how to assemble a pocket disguise kit you can carry with you and use at any time; ways to change your face, body shape, voice, mannerisms, even fingerprints; mail order sources for make-up, wigs, elevator shoes, fake eyeglasses, and much more. More than 130 detailed drawings. Learn to disguise yourself so completely even old friends won't recognize you! *1993, 5½ x 8½, 264 pp, illustrated, soft cover.* **$17.95.**

☐ **55072 The Muckraker's Manual, How To Do Your Own Investigative Reporting,** *by M. Harry.* How to dig out the dirt on anyone! Written for investigative reporters exposing political corruption, the detailed professional investigative techniques are useful to any investigation. Developing "inside" sources; Getting documents; Incredible ruses that really work; Interviewing techniques; Infiltration; When to stop an investigation; Protecting your sources; And much more. *1984, 5½ x 8½, 148 pp, illustrated, soft cover.* **$14.95.**

And much, much more! We offer the very finest in controversial and unusual books — please turn to our catalog ad on the next page.

LOOMPANICS UNLIMITED
PO BOX 1197
PORT TOWNSEND, WA 98368

CS96

Please send me the titles I have checked above. I have enclosed $_____ which includes $4.95 for the shipping and handling for the first $20.00 ordered. Please include $1.00 extra for each additional $20.00 ordered. (Washington residents please include 7.9% sales tax.)

Name_____

Address_____

City_____

State/Zip_____

We accept Visa and MasterCard. To place a credit card order *only,* call 1-800-380-2230, 9am to 4 pm, PDT, Monday through Friday.